Watered Down
Or
Washed Clean?

Dr. Kevin L. Thomas
Editors: Melissa Thomas &
Hannah Thomas

Dedication

To Melissa, my wife, my partner, my lover, and my very best friend. Thank you for your patience while I write, for reading and editing my work, for challenging my ideas, and most importantly for believing in me. Thank you for taking this journey with me!

To my son Michael, my daughter Katherine and her wife Hannah, and my daughter Olivia. You've taught me more about God than seminary did. The life of preacher's kids can be tough. You've handled it gracefully. I'm a blessed man to have you as my kids!

To Forest Lake United Methodist Church. Thank you for providing a home for my family. Thank you for the way you work for God's kingdom and encourage me to do the same. Thank you for showing up each week to gracefully listen to whatever God has put on my heart.

To those who have been hurt by church, and to those who think church doesn't matter, God still loves you as a precious child. Even if you've had difficulty finding your place in church, I pray that you will find your place in Christ.

About This Book

This book is based on two sermon series that I preached at Forest Lake United Methodist Church in Tuscaloosa, Alabama. To make it suitable for print, I've reworded most of the text, and I've included material that was not a part of the sermons. While I invite you to read through the entire book in order, each chapter stands alone. If one topic interests you more than another, feel free to skip ahead. To facilitate your reading, I've included scripture passages and a brief topic statement for each chapter in the Table of Contents.

Chapter One, "Watered Down," is an introduction to the two series and includes some autobiographical information which I hope you find helpful.

Part One, "10 Ways We Water Down the Gospel," will highlight ten of the ways that we sometimes misuse scripture and how those interpretations are harmful to others and to our kingdom work. You will likely find at least some of them surprising. This series is based on a blog post by Dr. Benjamin Corey in which he delineates these ten ways of watering down the Gospel. The framework is his, and I am grateful for his insight and for the inspiration for me to write my sermons.

Part Two, "Washed Clean," is a series based on the United Methodist baptismal vows. In this section, we'll explore the radical promises we make to Christ as we are initiated into the faith.

I hope this book encourages you and challenges you. Please feel free to interact with it. Agree. Disagree. Argue. Debate. Throw it across the room if it'll help. I humbly pray that God will use it and your reactions to it to draw you another step closer to God's amazing, loving presence.

Note: All scripture passages are in the New Revised Standard Version unless otherwise noted.

Table of Contents

#6: We Water Down the Gospel When We Tell People It's Clear and Simple—61
Matthew 22:36-40
The Bible makes almost nothing clear and simple.

#5 We Water Down the Gospel When We Eliminate the Centrality of Social Justice—77
Micah 6:6-8
There is no Good News without social justice.

#4: We Water Down the Gospel When We Explain Away Nonviolent Love of Enemies—89
Matthew 5:43-48
The distinguishing characteristic of Christ followers is how we love one another.

#3: We Water Down the Gospel When We Overemphasize Rarely Mentioned Sins—97
II Timothy 3:14-17
We often major in the minors while neglecting the things that truly matter to God.

#2: We Water Down the Gospel When We Exclusively Use the Concept of Penal Substitution--107
Isaiah 53:1-5
God the Father conspired with Jesus to provide a ransom for creation and to make Christ Victor.

Part One:
10 Ways We
Water Down
The Gospel

Watered Down

"You're watering down the Gospel!" The religious right levels the attack against those who are soft on sin, light on literalism, and equivocal on inerrancy. I know the tactic well, because for years it was mine. Being sure of all the Bible had to say on a vast array of issues, I stood ready to issue a verdict. If someone was open to the idea of reproductive rights, I dismissed the idea as disregarding scripture. When people considered inclusion of LGBTQ people, they were watering down the Gospel. As a twenty-something preacher, I lived in a black and white world—until I started seeing the gray.

As a young preacher, I adopted the label of my mentors—conservative evangelical. According to my definition, conservatives adhered to a strict interpretation of scripture. "God said it. That settles it." Evangelicals actively worked to spread the Gospel in the world. In reality, in connecting the two terms, I committed to spreading *my* strict interpretation of scripture in the world. My efforts were more to convince people of my way of thinking than to persuade them of the all-encompassing grace of Christ.

In my world, conservative evangelicals were good. Liberals were obviously bad for their loose interpretation of Scripture. Fundamentalists were, at least, almost as bad because of *their* legalism. It really bothered me that fundamentalists had lists of rules to follow and behaviors to be monitored. To me, it seemed they had a litmus test for Christianity. I was blind to the fact that what bothered me about fundamentalists was true of me. I claimed to be conservative evangelical, in practice I was a fundamentalist, and for me the fundamentals included

- Jesus is the Son of God.
- God created the world in 6 24-hour days.
- Evolution was a lie.
- God flooded the entire earth for 120 days.
- A giant fish really swallowed Jonah.
- God will punish you for drinking alcohol and cussing.
- God hates abortion.
- God hates homosexuality.
- And, finally, God generally agrees with me on most other topics.

Although I would never admit it, I was a fundamentalist, and if you disagreed with my list, I doubted your Christianity. At best, you were watering down the Gospel.

I'm eternally grateful to the people who loved me through this period in my life. To be so right about so many things at such an early age can make a person obnoxious. Churches showed me incredible grace in allowing me to serve, supporting me, and loving me deeply in spite of some of my unloving attitudes.

It was actually my conservative approach to scripture that led to the first chinks in my fundamentalist armor. If God really said it, and it's really settled, then some things were bothering me that I couldn't explain.

- If the Bible only accounts for about 6000 years of human (and cosmological) history, then what am I to do with human remains that are tens of thousands of years old? What am I to do with fossils that are millions of years old? How do I explain the starlight that I see that left its star hundreds of thousands of years ago? To be my kind of fundamentalist required rejecting science! Scientists had to be wrong—about almost everything! Yet, I still trusted doctors when I got sick.

- My fundamentalism taught me that homosexuality is an abomination—which is somehow worse than *ordinary* sins like murder and stealing. As a straight man who had no relationships with anyone who was openly homosexual (I wonder why), it didn't bother me to cast them in such an evil light. But, then I began to question why other things were abominations like eating shrimp and oysters and catfish. Really? God used the same horrible word to describe homosexuals and people who eat catfish? Maybe I was missing something important!

- Jesus messed up my rules about alcohol when He made 30 gallons of good wine at a wedding feast. I tried to explain that it was non-alcoholic wine. Then, it bothered me as a strict conservative that I was choosing *my* interpretation over what clearly God had said. It's interesting what mental gymnastics fundamentalists will go through to make the Bible agree with them.

- Plenty of scriptural passages just didn't add up to the Biblical inerrancy that was demanded by my fundamentalism.
  - The final word on diet is in Acts 15 where Gentile Christians are forbidden from eating meat with the blood still in it.
  - Paul forbids lawsuits.
  - Greed is one of the two most denounced sins in scripture. Yet, in our affluent culture we celebrate greed. We pastors use it to measure success— bigger church, bigger salary, bigger staff, and bigger house.
  - Later in the book, I'll share a list of 20 Bible verses Christians don't believe.
- Finally, experience began to teach me that my interpretation of scripture was wrong in too many places. Eventually, I began to make friends with some LGBTQ persons. Among them I discovered deeply committed Christians with devotional lives richer than mine. I observed them using their gifts in ministry in ways that moved everyone around them. I saw gay ministers reaching more people for Christ than I ever will. Regardless of what I thought the scriptures said, God was working in and through these people that I had excluded. My experience of real people took

me back to Acts 15:8-9, "And God, who knows the human heart, testified to them by giving them the Holy Spirit, just as he did to us; and in cleansing their hearts by faith he has made no distinction between them and us." I had an experience not unlike Peter's in Acts 10 where I heard God speak to my heart, "Do not call unclean what I have cleaned!" Through these lessons and so many others, my conservative approach to scripture convinced me that it was not the liberals, but I who was watering down the Gospel. By trying to force the Bible to be what it was not designed to be, by placing on it the burden of inerrancy, by making it a rulebook or an owner's manual, and by failing to see scripture as both divine and human, I was watering down the Gospel.

My favorite blogger, Dr. Benjamin Corey, sometimes tells my story better than I can tell it myself. Often, I read his words and find him saying what I felt but failed to put into words. You can find his blog here: https://www.patheos.com/blogs/formerlyfundie/. A couple of years ago, one of his blogs listed 10 ways we water down the Gospel https://www.benjaminlcorey.com/watering-down-the-gospel/. I found my formerly fundamental self, time and again, as I read through his list. I adapted the list into a sermon series which I shared with my congregation at Forest Lake United Methodist Church in Tuscaloosa, Alabama. Some of my members requested that I turn the series into a book, and these pages are my attempt at completing that task. During Part One, we'll count down the 10 Ways We Water Down the Gospel, David Letterman style. Each sermon will highlight one of the ways that American

Christianity sometimes misses the point. Then, in Part Two, I'll share another sermon series, this one on the United Methodist Baptismal vows. In those three sermons, "Repent," "Resist," and "Confess," we'll explore what those vows really require of us.

Perhaps the greatest strength that I bring to this book is not my knowledge or training but the realization that I don't have it figured out. Over-confidence was the sin of my youth. Then, I had all the right answers. Now, I know that I don't even understand the questions. Behind my desk in my study is a picture of the universe taken by the Hubble Telescope. On the picture is an inset of planet Earth with a line drawn deep into a cluster of galaxies. The caption for the inset reads, "You Are Here." That picture is a constant reminder to me of the size of our God. I do believe that God created this vast universe that's over 6 trillion miles in diameter. A God who can do that is far beyond the wildest imaginations of my feeble mind. So, I push back against ideas that limit divine activity to human understanding. I embrace the mystery of a God I can't comprehend, and I invite you to join me on a journey in discovering ways we've watered down the Gospel and limited the God who washed us clean. And, now, we'll begin the countdown with #10…

#10: We Water Down the Gospel When We Try to Live it Out in Isolation

I Corinthians 12:12-20
12 For just as the body is one and has many members, and all the members of the body, though many, are one body, so it is with Christ. 13 For in the one Spirit we were all baptized into one body—Jews or Greeks, slaves or free—and we were all made to drink of one Spirit. 14 Indeed, the body does not consist of one member but of many. 15 If the foot would say, "Because I am not a hand, I do not belong to the body," that would not make it any less a part of the body. 16 And if the ear would say, "Because I am not an eye, I do not belong to the body," that would not make it any less a part of the body. 17 If the whole body were an eye, where would the hearing be? If the whole body were hearing, where would the sense of smell be? 18 But as it is, God arranged the members in the body, each one of them, as he chose. 19 If all were a single member, where would the body be? 20 As it is, there are many members, yet one body.

Prayer
Loving God, Father, Son, and Holy Spirit, you live in eternal community, and you invite us to participate in that divine relationship. Forgive us for

the ways we isolate ourselves. Teach us to live in communion not only with those with whom we agree but also with those with whom we disagree, and even with those who are outside of our faith tradition. Teach us how to live and love in harmony. Amen.

We live with an ever-present temptation to live our faith in isolation, to separate the secular from the sacred, to compartmentalize our faith into multiple cubbyholes. I saw one clear example of that tendency 15 years ago while teaching a Bible class for a group of high school juniors in a Christian school. Several of my students played on the school's football team. During one of our classes, I shared the importance of living our faith all week long, everywhere we go. I suggested to them that we should follow Christ equally on Sunday mornings, Friday nights, and Saturday afternoons. After all, Paul instructs us to do everything as if we were doing it for the Lord (Colossians 3:23). For my "inside the church" world view, the suggestion seemed far from radical. Several of my students pushed back against the idea rather strongly, leading to an exchange that probably educated me more than them.

"I don't think that'll work," said one player in the class.

More interested in proving my point than listening, I countered, "God calls us to be faithful to Christ in *everything*!"

My student replied, "We're football players. We want to win ballgames. We can't be thinking about following Christ while we're on the football field. Jesus has to stay on the sideline!"

He was serious, and his fellow students agreed. In their mindset, there was no room for Jesus in the violent, competitive setting of a football game. They saw Christ as a liability, an obstacle in their game plan. Now, I'm not attacking football, nor do I claim that these few students are representative of everyone who puts on a helmet, but they were sharing their opinions honestly. They became *my* teacher, highlighting for this career preacher the real-life difficulties of following Christ.

Their story reminds me of one I heard about the Crusaders. I can't prove the anecdote true, but its lesson is valid. There was a time in history when the church fielded an army whose purpose was to violently take possession of the Holy Land. The soldiers in that army were called Crusaders. As the story goes, when Crusaders were baptized, they had a custom of holding their sword arms up out of the water while the rest of their bodies were immersed with Christ. The symbolism carried their message. "Jesus can have the rest of me, but the devil's keeping my sword arm." The implication is that, in the heat of battle, the devil is a better ally than the Prince of Peace. Baptismal vows might interfere with the violence of their mission. Jesus had to stay on the sideline.

More recently, I was teaching in one of my previous churches on the subject of vocation. Based on Colossians 3:23 and the principle of doing everything as for the Lord, I made my case that our daily jobs should be offered in service to Christ. I was elevating the holiness of work. To be honest, I was thinking about doctors, nurses, teachers, social workers, people who design and build things, and people who do so much to order our lives. (I'd not learned the lesson my high school football students tried to teach me.) After my sermon, one of my church members approached me.

"I agree with the idea of what you're saying," my friend told me, "but I do have a real problem with it."

I was a little surprised that my friend was challenging me on a point I'd made so clearly. After all, my doctoral dissertation was on Vocation. Surely, I had offered expert opinion. I answered him, "Really? What could be the problem with doing your daily job for Christ?"

"I work for the department of defense," he told me. "I spend my days making missiles designed to kill people. I can't figure out how to do that job for Jesus."

Once again, I became the student. I didn't have an answer for my friend. Years later, I still don't have a good recommendation for how to make instruments of war in the name of Jesus.

Honestly, many things in our lives tempt us to compartmentalize. We face obstacles that tempt us to exclaim, "No, there's no room for Jesus, here," whether it's what we do on Monday morning, or Friday night, or those times when no one is looking. We live with a very real temptation to isolate our faith into certain acceptable quadrants while erecting secular divisions in which we can do whatever we please.

When we isolate our faith, we're watering down the Gospel! When we divide our worlds into secular and sacred, we are diluting the message of Christ. John Wesley, the founder of the Methodist Movement, put it this way, "There is no holiness apart from social holiness." Very often, that quote is used to support justice ministries, but there's more to it. While Wesley was a staunch advocate for social justice, his intent in these words is that the Christian faith must be lived socially, in community. Christians don't generally achieve holiness by secluding themselves in the desert, but by learning to follow Christ in the messiness of daily life. We grow in Christ where our spiritual lives intersect with real people. God may call some to live separate lives in prayer, meditation, and writing, but for most of us, spiritual formation will happen in real world settings with everyday people. We'll have to learn how to let Christ live into every aspect of daily life. Daily challenges become schools for the soul, like when a car pulls out in front of you, or when people run over you with shopping carts. It's those times when we want to offer a few creative suggestions for what to do with that WWJD bracelet that actually give us real-life opportunities to practice following Jesus.

We American Christians shy away from the social aspect of Christianity. We prefer an individualistic approach where salvation is all about Jesus and me. I recall one church member who openly espoused that sentiment. While serving his church, I invited him to be a part of an accountability group in which members would weekly inquire about each other's practice of classic Christian disciplines. My church member responded bluntly to my invitation. "Pastor, my faith is a private matter between God and me. It's none of your business!" While I understood his position, I shared with him what I would share with anyone. His position does not represent scriptural Christianity. He didn't want to hear that. We may not, either. A private faith is more convenient but less fruitful. "There is no holiness apart from social holiness."

I'm aware that some people have little choice about isolation. Thousands of people live alone with little opportunity for interaction with other people. As I write these words, I'm experiencing some of that loneliness during the COVID-19 pandemic that strives to separate people from one another. God will not punish us or stunt our spiritual growth due to isolation beyond our control! If you have little opportunity to interact with others, God is still with you, and God still invites you to be in relationship with others, at least, through prayer. While I've been separated recently from those I love, I've found greater opportunity and desire to be in prayer for those people. God, who lives in community, will provide the community of the Trinity to those whom this world has isolated!

God is love. Biblical Christianity is rooted in our love for God and our love for others. We only learn love in community. It's very easy for me to love someone with whom I never interact. I can easily love my enemies as long as they're on the other side of the world or tucked safely behind some border. When people do get close enough to us to bother us, we resort to a tired, worn-out cop-out, "Love the sinner. Hate the sin." I'm beginning to wonder how much time we've spent with the "sinner." Have we really done the work to build a relationship with the "sinner?" Or, are we so obsessed with the "sin" that we can't even see the "sinner?" Can we truly claim to love the "sinner" if we haven't spent time in relationship with them? Jesus always seemed to be more concerned with the person than with the sin.

I'm convinced that God intentionally allows obstinate people into our lives. God blesses us with obnoxious people! Anyone can love pleasant people.

Everyone enjoys the company of friends, but Christians don't get credit for only having that kind of love. "For if you love those who love you, what reward do you have? Do not even the tax collectors do the same? And if you greet only your brothers and sisters, what more are you doing than others? Do not even the Gentiles do the same?" (Matthew 5:46-47). Jesus calls us to love our enemies and pray for people who persecute us. So, God allows obnoxious people in our lives to teach us that kind of love. Dale Galloway calls those people EGRs, Extra Grace Required. EGRs teach us how to love like Jesus. Maybe it's the crazy uncle that no one wants to come to Thanksgiving. He's there to give you the opportunity to learn how to love. People in my ministry who have opposed me, my enemies, have taught me how to love. I've had the opportunity to provide pastoral care for people who have lied about me. I've been with them in the hospital. I've wept with their families at their funerals. I've had the opportunity to love addicts without getting engulfed in their additions. I've learned to love victims without becoming a victim, myself. The only way those things can happen is by entering into a deep relationship with people. It's easy to claim to love. It's harder to live a loving lifestyle.

One of the essential building blocks of Methodism was the Class Meeting, a group of about a dozen men and women who met weekly to inquire of one another's souls. These meetings were not Bibles studies, worship services, Sunday school classes, or prayer meetings. There was no lecture, no teaching. Class Meetings gathered weekly for members to ask probing questions of one another.

- How is it with your soul?

- When have you been tempted in the last week?
- How did you fail?
- How did you overcome?
- When did you experience the presence of Christ in the last week?

Each person gave an honest account of his or her Christian journey for the previous week. Christianity happened in community. The result was a revival that swept across two continents. Social holiness changes the world!

When we try to live the faith in isolation, we're watering down the Gospel. We are designed to do this thing together! In I Corinthians, Paul describes the church as a single body with many members. We will not do well in life as an ear unless we're connected to the rest of the body. Being a hand is useless if we're not connected to a wrist that connects to an arm that's attached to the rest of the body. In the same way, Christians must be connected to each other to flourish, or maybe even survive, in the Christian faith.

There's more! It's not just about the church! In John 3:16, Jesus teaches us that God loved the entire world so much that God sent Jesus into the world that the world might be saved through Him! You and I, together, are the body of Christ. God is still sending Christ into the world for the redemption of the world. We have the great privilege of continuing Jesus' ministry—everyday, everywhere. We don't have the option of a sacred/secular divide. Christ is all and in all and invites us to be present as His body in *every* part of human experience.

I've discovered real joy in having sacred conversations in what are considered to be secular spaces. Jesus went to parties in the homes of sinners and outcasts. The religious leaders called it a scandal. He went anyway. He invites us to follow. Thirty-one million Americans have left the church, some because the church hurt them. Others just decided we aren't relevant. We can't wait on them to return to our sanctuaries. We can meet them in "secular" spaces—restaurants, ballgames, parties, bars, all the places where people hang out. If we are the Body of Christ, we must be the Body of Christ in the world, because that's where Jesus went.

We also need to be honest when we gather. One of the most common complaints non-Christians have of church folks is that we're hypocrites. They're right. We are! But, let's be clear about the definition. Hypocrisy is not what happens when we make mistakes. It's what happens when we pretend that we don't. Non-Christians are not critical of us for failing as much as they are critical of our pretense that we have it all together. What makes us hypocrites is that we pretend to be perfect. We act holy on Sunday morning. Then they see our Monday morning version, and our faith looks phony. We yell at one another in the car on the way to church and then put on phony smiles as we enter the sanctuary. Our acting job stunts our spiritual growth and it harms those who are watching. In order to grow, we must start where we are. We must be honest. Before we invite the unchurched to come as they are, we must come as we are! If the church is being the church, we shouldn't have to hide

- When we're struggling with our marriage,
- When our kids are in trouble,

- When addiction hits close to home,
- When our finances are in shambles,
- When our worlds are falling apart.

If the church doesn't understand and show grace, then when people have problems they run *away*! When a church understands and shows grace, and people have problems, they run *to* the church!

In the true Body of Christ, the one that Paul talks about in I Corinthians, it's safe to be real, to be who we really are. When Adam and Eve sinned, they felt that they had to hide from God. Jesus came into the world to find those who were hiding and to love them as they are. God is inviting you today to come out of the shadows. Tear down the sacred/secular divide. Let Jesus into every part of life. Discover the joy of community. Discover the joy of being fully loved.

#9 We Water Down the Gospel When We Make It About Changing Others

Matthew 7:1-5 (NRSV)

1 "Do not judge, so that you may not be judged. 2 For with the judgment you make you will be judged, and the measure you give will be the measure you get. 3 Why do you see the speck in your neighbor's eye, but do not notice the log in your own eye? 4 Or how can you say to your neighbor, 'Let me take the speck out of your eye,' while the log is in your own eye? 5 You hypocrite, first take the log out of your own eye, and then you will see clearly to take the speck out of your neighbor's eye.

Prayer

Lord Jesus, help us to hear your words. Give us courage to follow them. Teach us to love with gentleness so that we might also receive mercy. Help us to follow you in every way. Amen.

It's amazing how much we can see through a log. I did it for years. I was an expert. I could see straight through the log in my own eye, and I was more than willing to poke around in your eye trying to remove even the tiniest speck. No one wants to be on the receiving end of that probing judgment!

Everyone else could see how blind I was while trying to help others see clearly. Everyone could see the absurdity, except for me. As a young pastor, I was certain that it was *my* responsibility to point out sin, to correct those whose care was entrusted to me, and to set them on the right path (push them into *my* way of thinking). As a 21-year-old pastor, I was certain of what was wrong with everyone else. It's amazing how smart I was! (It's even more amazing to realize how much *less* I know after serving for 32 years in ministry. The longer I serve, the dumber I seem to get.) I had the "correct" Biblical answer for every controversial issue in society.

- Abortion
- Alcohol
- Homosexuality
- Tattoos
- Piercings
- Palm Readers
- Ouija Boards
- Horoscopes

I even had the "correct" Biblical opinion for the Teen-Age Mutant Ninja Turtles. I wish I were making all this stuff up! Sadly, if you could listen to sermons from my early years, you'd hear my condemnation for all these things, even the Ninja Turtles. I had an amazing ability to identify everyone's sin— everyone's but *mine*. Oblivious to the log in my own eye, I felt responsible to poke at the specks in others' eyes.

In my world, it was the pastor's job to point out people's faults, to be tough on sin. To be fair, we pastors get a lot of accolades for preaching hellfire and damnation sermons. People will pat us on the back for a tough stance against sin, as long as we don't mention *their* sin. Judgmentalism worked for me. The affirmation my churches gave me for my Biblical preaching fed my ego and shining the light on everyone else's sin kept the spotlight off my own. Judging others allowed me to live with the illusion that my life was fine just the way it was. It was others who needed to change, not me!

Judgement works like that. "The Bible calls what *they're* doing an abomination. I would never do that. So, I must be okay." It's a very unhealthy short-cut to a perverted illusion of holiness! It's a Biblical excuse to isolate ourselves from the people that we hate. There's nothing right about that way of thinking, but church folks have been thinking that way for years.

Poking around at other people's specks is harmful. Judgment destroys. Spiritual superiority grants us false permission to be hateful with fellow human beings. I said some really hurtful things in those years. I used the pulpit to assault people with whom I disagreed. Preaching to a church crowd in rural Alabama, I remember making the statement, "If God doesn't punish San Francisco for their homosexuality, He owes Sodom and Gomorrah an apology." I even went further saying that I wished California would fall off into the Pacific Ocean, because, apparently, California was the origin of all sin. I said hateful things about women who had had abortions, even calling them murderers. I attacked people with tattoos and too many piercings, though I never could definitively prove how many was too many. These "sins" were easy targets in my rural, elderly congregation. I got to be "tough" on sin without offending people in the room. I roped them into my own illusion. We're okay. It's all of *those* people that are the sinners. *We* don't have to worry about change. I'm embarrassed to write these words. I've had to repent and apologize to quite a few people. I carry with me the shame of these acts. I wish, with all my heart, that I could undo them. I can't. But, what I can do is stand in solidarity with those I used to attack. I choose, now, to be for them. I choose to love.

Because hate does too much damage. It hurts those we attack, and it hurts us, as well. Jesus actually lets us pick the way we'll be measured. We get to write the key by which we will be graded. The way that we judge will determine the way we are judged (Matthew 7:2). I'm glad that I didn't die when I was 21. If God would have judged me the way that I judged others, there would have been no hope for me. The thought of facing the same harsh judgment I doled out to others petrifies me. If we're really taking the Bible seriously, Christians should be the most graceful, merciful, forgiving people in the world if for no other reason that self-preservation. I sure want God to be gentle with me when it's my turn to be judged, so I should learn to be gentle with those around me—even if I think they're wrong, maybe especially if I think they're wrong! When we're hateful of others, we hurt them and ourselves. Nobody wins!

We water down the Gospel when we try to change others without first changing ourselves, when we use the Bible as a weapon to attack those we don't want to love. Too often, we make up our minds, we follow our prejudices, and then search for Biblical support for our hateful opinions, just like we've done with the story of Sodom and Gomorrah. People who choose to hate LGBTQIA+ persons appeal to this story from Genesis to support their hatred. God sends two angels to Sodom to rescue Abraham's nephew Lot and his family from the sinful city before God destroys it. While the male angels are in Lot's house, the men of the city threaten to break into Lot's house so they can rape the two angels. Had that crime occurred, it would have been a same-sex *rape*. If you see this story as proof that committed, loving same-sex relationships are wrong, then you're misusing scripture to justify your own hatred! The story is about a violent sexual act that no loving person supports. Furthermore, the prophet Ezekiel weighs in on the story. "This was the guilt of your sister Sodom: she and her daughters had pride, excess of food, and prosperous ease, but did not aid the poor and needy" (Ezekiel 16:49). Greed is the new sodomy! Who knew? Very few preachers will want to preach that Biblical sermon! Rather than believing the Bible, people choose to misuse the Bible to support their hatred of LGBTQIA+ persons. We water down the Gospel when we use the Bible to try to change others without allowing it to change us. It's like when my church members tell me after a sermon, "Oh, I have a friend who really needs to hear what you said." Too often we perceive God's message as for someone else when God is really trying to get through to us.

Paul got it. He called himself the chief of sinners. That statement makes a lot of us Christians uncomfortable. Paul was an Apostle, authored 2/3 of the New Testament and planted churches throughout the known world. If he called himself chief of sinners, what does that say about the rest of us? We try to play it off as humility or even false humility, but what if there's more to it? Paul understood that Christ followers are supposed to be so aware of their own sin that they must be gentle with other people's sins. The idea is reflected in the Sermon on the Mount. "Blessed are the merciful, for they will receive mercy" (Matthew 5:7). Paul interpreted his own sin as the worst, and still, God forgave him. Paul knew that same forgiveness for him, the chief of sinners, must be available to everyone else. When we recognize how big the log is in our own eyes, we begin to hope and trust that specks in people's eyes don't disqualify them from grace. If the people with the specks can't be forgiven, there's no hope for me. Paul got it!

Neither Paul nor Jesus is calling us to ignore sin. Sin separates us from one another and from God. It violates the law of love. Sin is a failure to love. I didn't understand that truth while I was blinded by hatred. As long as I had such a big log in my eye, I could only define sin by a set of some arbitrary moral standards. I was like the Pharisees accusing Jesus of sinning by healing on the Sabbath, when, in fact, Jesus was loving by healing on the Sabbath. Hateful hearts only see broken rules and fail to see the beauty of love.

Fortunately, over the last 30 years, God has been changing my heart. I didn't have an all-at-once Damascus road type of experience. Rather, during those decades my simple answers stopped working. The black and white began to turn gray.

For years, I taught that homosexuality is wrong, because the Bible says so. During all that time, I never had a relationship with anyone who was openly gay. In retrospect, I'm not surprised. Few LGBTQIA+ people would have felt safe around me, given my hateful opinions. Finally, a couple of relationships caused me to rethink my opinion and reconsider what I thought the Bible said.

For a week one July, my family tent camped on Lake Martin in our hometown of Alexander City, Alabama. By sheer luck or by Providence, the camper next to our tent was occupied by a lesbian couple and their son. In my mind, at the time, they were living an evil lifestyle. They represented all that was wrong in our country—except that they didn't. They were kind, peaceful, and loving (fruits of the Spirit for those keeping score). They were generous with us. Even though they knew I was a pastor and disapproved of them, the invited us to share the resources their camper had that our tent did not. They were incredibly gracious (another Christian characteristic). By the end of the week, I had come to the uncomfortable realization that our lesbian neighbors had actually been more Christ-like than I had been.

A second encounter came when a church member asked if I would provide pastoral counseling for friends of hers, a lesbian couple who was having relationship issues. I'm still not sure why my church member felt I would be open to the idea. I reluctantly agreed as a favor to her. At a loss for how to proceed, I sought the counsel of some conservative colleagues. One responded, "First, tell them to stop being gay!" That approach just didn't seem right, certainly not Christian! I met with the couple and found them to be delightful. There were having similar relationship struggles to opposite-sex couples I had counseled. They were working at loving each other better. At the end of our time together, I had no legitimate reason to say their relationship was wrong simply because they were of the same gender.

John Wesley had a practical approach to Biblical interpretation. If he interpreted the Bible one way, but plain experience taught him something else, he assumed that his interpretation was wrong. My experiences were leading me to believe that my interpretations of scripture might actually be wrong— a huge blow to my even bigger pride.

Reality began to challenge other Biblical interpretations. As a high schooler, I adopted a strong pro-life position (although now I might refer to it as an anti-abortion position). It's a fairly easy stance for a guy who is not sexually active to take. (Again, you see the tendency to judge sins we don't commit.) I even wore a lapel pin that featured the feet of a 12-week-old fetus. As I shared earlier in this chapter, I regretfully referred to women who had had abortions as murderers. One of those women had the incredible courage to confront me. She shared with me the pain in that decision and the pain and guilt that my sermon had added to her. Perhaps for the first time, I discovered the harm done by my preaching. Still, I protected myself with the claim that my delivery was wrong, but my position was still right.

Then, my church hosted a program led by a crisis pregnancy center. One of the girls they served was 11 years old. A pregnant 11-year-old! My convictions about abortion exploded! How can anyone offer a simple solution to the pregnancy of an 11-year-old girl. Black and white morphed into gray right before my self-righteous eyes. Years later, it still baffles me that male politicians think they have the right answer for that girl's situation.

A related topic and object of my attacks was pre-marital sex. During my years in youth ministry, I was a part of a culture that treated virginity as the ultimate virtue and pre-marital sex as the unforgiveable sin. Christianity was defined by an intact hymen! I saw way too many young people leave the church because they had failed our test. No one wanted sexually active teens in our youth groups. So, they left, and most have never come back. Still others, wanting to remain in church, chose abortion to hide the fact that they had been "promiscuous." I go into greater detail about the damage done by the purity cult in my book, *The Immoral Christian*. Our fear of sexuality is driving people away from church, and worse, away from God.

Sitting at a church function with a female church member, we overheard another preacher explain that the problem with the church these days was women with too many piercings. My church member had three in one ear and two in the other. I guess my colleague had answered the question, "How many is too many?" I knew the woman to be a devout Christian regardless of the number of holes in her body!

I've met Christians that sport tattoos. Church folks like to remind them that the body is the temple of the Holy Spirit. One tatted-up friend responded that her temple has stained-glass windows. Some of my friends with tattoos are far more effective in ministry than I'll ever be.

Real people with real, beautiful lives clashed with my interpretations and my preconceived notions. To be honest, my interpretations died a slow painful death. When your super-power is being a nerd, it's hard to admit you're wrong. Eventually, the truth shined through my phony Biblical interpretations, and it's still shining, because I still have a lot to learn.

Of this I'm sure, we must love God and others, all others! Billy Graham put it like this, "It's the Holy Spirit's job to convict, God's job to judge, and my job to love." I cannot forget that God forgave my hatefulness and graciously revealed to me the places where I was wrong. I can only offer that same forgiveness to others, but it'll be up to the Holy Spirit to point out errors. Christ was gentle with me. I choose to be gentle with others.

With Christ's help, we can do better. We can invite change in others, too, but only by loving them as Christ loves us. It was Christ's love that changed me. It's the only thing that I hope will change others. How arrogant that I used to believe others should change to suit *my* opinions. People should only be molded by the love of God!

It's as simple and as complicated as that, and I'm still trying to figure it out. Loving people can be hard work. We'll need God's help. God does call us to change the world, but not by accusing people of evil or judging others' behaviors. He calls us to change the world by demonstrating God's love and forgiveness in such a life-giving way that people are attracted to Christ. It's not when we put people down that they are attracted to Christ, but when we raise them up!

#8 We Water Down the Gospel When We Make it Sound Easy

Matthew 8:19-22

19 A scribe then approached and said, "Teacher, I will follow you wherever you go." 20 And Jesus said to him, "Foxes have holes, and birds of the air have nests; but the Son of Man has nowhere to lay his head." 21 Another of his disciples said to him, "Lord, first let me go and bury my father." 22 But Jesus said to him, "Follow me, and let the dead bury their own dead."

Prayer

Almighty God, open our eyes to see the road set before us. Equip us and prepare us for the sometimes difficult task of following you. Help us to desire more than an escape from hell. Give us perseverance for the long journey that leads to life. Amen.

The revival preachers of my childhood always made it sound so simple. First, they painted this horribly vivid picture of hell with people tormented for eternity in a lake of fire. The preacher said that there would be weeping and gnashing of teeth. I never found anyone who knew how to gnash your teeth, but it certainly sounded unpleasant. As the sermon wore on, the evangelist did all within his power to convince us that this horrible fate was ours because of all the sin in our lives. Finally, he'd come to our rescue with an offer no one could refuse. To escape this fiery destiny, all we had to do was bow our heads, close our eyes, raise our hands, and repeat the "sinner's prayer" as the preacher lined it out to us. After praying the prayer, he always asked us to come to the altar for more prayer. What an incredible promise! All the torment of hell washed away by repeating a few magic words! It sounded incredibly enticing! A few words mumbled under my breath could provide eternal fire insurance. A short walk to the altar could punch my ticket to heaven. As if the preacher needed one more hook to draw us to the altar, he often added the phrase, "No strings attached." What more could you want? The preacher offered a ticket to heaven for a prayer and nothing more. Of course, I prayed the prayer—many times! Time and again I heard the message. Each time I heard it, I didn't feel that I was any different from the last time I prayed the prayer. So, each time I dutifully bowed my head, closed my eyes, raised my hand, and repeated the words, again. After all, there was a lot to gain, and there were no strings attached. (By the way, all of those raised hands sure made the preacher's numbers look good, and, yes, preachers do count, report, and occasionally exaggerate those numbers.)

Deep down inside, something didn't feel right. Even as a child, I wrestled with the idea of a faith that's so transactional. It didn't make sense that God only wanted a few words from me. It didn't make sense that my salvation occurred in a few minutes, and that all that was left was to wait a few decades to go to heaven. I absolutely believe in free grace, but instead I was offered cheap grace that promises a reward without asking for anything. Jesus didn't make it that easy!

As I grew older, the message expanded. Preachers went from peddling tickets to heaven to promising all sorts of services that God would provide. According to some of the people I followed, God not only wanted to give me heaven in exchange for a few words, but also wanted to make life easy on earth by providing financial stability, perfect health, and all-around easy living. Again, they offered this life on easy street at a bargain. All I needed was faith.

In reality, life was challenging during my early years as a pastor. Melissa and I had our first child in 1990 while I was serving my first two churches in Winfield, Alabama and attending seminary in Memphis. The bills added up quickly: tuition, books, fees, gasoline (for the 172 mile one way commute to school), rent, utilities for two homes, medical bills, diapers, formula, and food for my wife and me. My salary at the time was $11,000/year. The paycheck ran out long before the bills. We were just starting out, and we were already drowning in debt. It was during that stressful time that I distinctly remember listening to a preacher on TV. He said that he knew some of us faced financial troubles. We did. He said that God wanted us to be debt free, that God was prepared to pay off all our bills. Then, the televangelist told me to go get my bills. (He waited for us to get them.) Next, he said to lay one hand on our bills and the other hand on the TV screen. His whole pitch sounded crazy, but when you're desperate, you'll try almost anything. He prayed that

God would pay off our debts. Finally, he said that all we needed to do to be debt free is to "sow" some money into his ministry. Send him and check and God would pay our debt. I wasn't buying that! If the preacher knew how to get God to pay off debts, why was he asking for my money anyway? At least he did admit that there were strings attached. When you're drowning in debt, it's easy to believe God wants to pay your bills. But, did Jesus really promise an easy life?

Other preachers offered the opportunity to walk in divine health. For them, God's actions in our lives include healing and even the power to avoid sickness. Their message is simple, "If you have faith, you won't get sick. You'll walk in divine health. But, if by some strange chance you do get sick, just pray, and God will heal. God promised health," they said, "and God honors His word. We just have to hold Him to it!" I wish I were exaggerating, but this is the exact argument that people have presented to me over and over.

I want to be careful on this topic. I do believe that Jesus touched the sick and healed them. I believe that God continues to heal, today, in both ordinary and miraculous means. I've experienced miraculous healing in my own life, and I've experienced healing at the hands of doctors who have been gifted by God to restore health. I lay hands on people, and I pray for their healing. Sometimes, the person recovers. Sometimes, I do their funeral.

You've probably had similar experiences. Perhaps you've prayed diligently for a loved one to be healed. Maybe, the person got better. But, if you've been praying for people for long, you've also experienced those that didn't get better. They died.

Your prayers seemed unanswered. In those times, we search for explanations. We want to know why our prayers failed. We want to know where God was, why God didn't "honor His word."

But, God didn't promise an easy life. God never promised perpetual health. In fact, God promised that hard times would come on all of us. I'm writing this chapter while under a 24-hour/day curfew in an effort to slow the COVID-19 pandemic. The current crisis is not God's failure to answer prayer, nor is it God's judgement for bad behavior. Sickness is part of the human experience. Prosperity preachers and divine healers offer a simple formula to exempt us from this part of the human experience, but there is no formula. There's no certainty in healing. There's no recipe for divine health, and the faith healers know it! If what they preach were true, they'd be walking the halls of our hospitals rather than filling auditoriums. They would clear out intensive care units rather than filling civic centers!

Yes, God heals! But, God is in charge of healing, not us, and God never promised that the Christian life would be illness free.

Sometimes, the promises people make for God are absolutely absurd. While attending a men's retreat in Georgia, I listened to a preacher make an outrageous promise of what God would do for us if we just have faith. He and his wife lived near Atlanta and occasionally had to go downtown on business. Parking in the inner city is always at a premium. So, the pastor and his wife prayed as they drove into town asking God to provide them a parking place right in front of the building to which they were going. They exercised their faith. He then claimed that they *always* get to park right in front of the building where they are going. "Sometimes," he continued, "we have to drive around the block a few times, but God always provides us a space." The preacher's fantastic story caused several problems for me.

- What did God do with the car that was parked in the preacher's spot? Did God cause the ground to open up and swallow some poor guy's Ford Fiesta? What offense or lack of faith must have caused the guy to lose his car?
- What is it about following Christ that should make a Christian *expect* the best parking spot? Didn't Jesus tell us, "The last shall be first and the first shall be last?" Doesn't Christian humility demand that we give preference to one another?
- Is it really an act of faith to reduce the God of the universe to a parking attendant?

That preacher's message was actually very beneficial to me (in addition to providing a good sermon story). He helped me to form a more reliable method for theological interpretation. If your theology promotes a God who serves you, then your theology probably misses the point, and your God is probably too small. In a healthy theology, we remember who God is and that our role is to glorify and serve God. One of Paul's most frequent ways of referring to himself was as a slave of Christ. Any theology that puts me first is, at best, misinformed, at worst, heretical.

Popular American Christianity promises life on easy street. If I haven't convinced you, yet, allow me to offer one more example. During my first six months as a pastor, I was completing my bachelor's degree at the University of Alabama, about an hour south of the two churches I served. Being a preacher,

I assumed that I should only listen to Christian radio. So, for my two-hour, round-trip commute, I dutifully listened to a Christian channel broadcast out of Birmingham, Alabama. My travel time happened to coincide with the station's teaching time. I got to listen to various radio preachers in 15-minute sound bites. It was okay with me. As a young preacher, I was eager to learn and since I had the new responsibility of preaching weekly, I was grateful for the sermon assistance I got. (It took me too long to discern how bad the assistance was.)

I still remember the lesson that one of my radio mentors preached during one of those trips to Tuscaloosa. He pointed out that during Creation, God gave people dominion "over the fish of the sea, and over the fowl of the air, and over the cattle, and over all the earth, and over every creeping thing that creepeth upon the earth" (Genesis 1:26). He told me that I had control over the animals. God said so. My radio mentor claimed that when he went fishing, he commanded the fish to get on his hook, because God gave him dominion over the fish. To be completely honest, as a young, arrogant preacher, I kind of liked the sound of that. Still, I was left wondering, if faith really works like that, then why even bait the hook? Why not just tell the fish to jump into the boat? The false promise of much of the American church is an easy, trouble free life *if* you have faith and will bow your heads, close your eyes, raise your hand, and repeat the magic words.

In the presence of so much prosperity theology, Jesus' words kept troubling me. Apparently ignorant of the promises made by televangelists, Jesus taught that discipleship was a hard life. "The Son of Man has no place to lay His head." "Follow me, and let the dead bury the dead." "Deny yourself. Take up your cross (implement of execution), and follow me." Jesus did not believe that following Him would be easy. To the contrary, He teaches clearly that a faithful life will cost everything. There are not just strings attached, but giant metal cables!

Life wasn't any easier for the earliest Christians. Just listen to the experiences of our spiritual forefathers and foremothers.

> 35 Women received their dead by resurrection. Others were tortured, refusing to accept release, in order to obtain a better resurrection. 36 Others suffered mocking and flogging, and even chains and imprisonment. 37 They were stoned to death, they were sawn in two, they were killed by the sword; they went about in skins of sheep and goats, destitute, persecuted, tormented— 38 of whom the world was not worthy. They wandered in deserts and mountains, and in caves and holes in the ground. (Hebrews 11:35-38)

Nothing about that life reminds me of the instruction I got from the Christian radio station. The earliest Christ followers sacrificed everything. Within only weeks after Jesus' crucifixion, Stephen, one of His earliest followers, was stoned to death while preaching a sermon about Jesus! A woman in one of my earlier churches who had bought into the prosperity Gospel told me that Stephen would not have died if he had just known to ask for help. According to her, poor Stephen was too ignorant to save his life. What a sad misrepresentation of discipleship! The Revelation tells of the only time that attention in heaven is diverted from the throne of

God. It's when the martyrs are honored. All of heaven turns to give respect to those who have given all for Christ.

We water down the Gospel when we make it sound like following Jesus is easy. "The greatest among you will be your servant" (Matthew 23:11). Mother Teresa became one of the best-known Christians in history because of her willingness to clean the wounds of lepers in Calcutta, India. Her greatness was not in mansions or salaries or divine health, but in her ability to see Christ in the face of the world's poorest people. If we dare to follow Christ, we can't claim to be more important than the One who stooped to wash His disciples' feet. Discipleship can be a long, difficult journey. It wasn't designed as an easy way out of hell.

In the "Sermon on the Mount," Jesus offered commandments that destroy any notion of Christian privilege and easy living. During the sermon, He never asked us to bow our heads or repeat after Him. He does offer a radical new way of living that comes with mighty big strings attached!

"If anyone forces you to go one mile, go also the second mile" (Matthew 5:41). Under First Century Roman law, a soldier could compel someone to carry the soldier's pack for a mile. Any self-respecting Jew would have hated this practice. Most Jews had witnessed a Roman soldier killing a friend or family member. They were a foreign, occupying force, and they were hated! Jesus' words are scandalous. "Do you want to follow Me?" asks Jesus. "Don't complain about carrying that soldier's pack for a mile, and to demonstrate the love of God, carry it an extra mile as well." Bend over backwards to serve your enemies. Discipleship is hard.

In the same sermon, Jesus says, "If anyone wants to sue you and take your coat, give your cloak as well" (Matthew 5:40). That's downright un-American! We're taught to fight for what's ours! Jesus reminds us that all we have is a gift from God and is available for God's purposes, even if those purposes include giving it away to someone who doesn't deserve it. We water down the Gospel when we make it sound like following Jesus is easy.

One of Jesus' most difficult sayings comes just before these two. "If anyone strikes you on the right cheek, turn the other also." Jesus can't really mean that, can He? Surely, I deserve to be treated better than that! Except, Jesus wasn't treated better. He suffered violence for our sakes. By what logic do we deserve better than Him?

Jesus wraps up this chapter with a passage that commands us to love our enemies and pray for those who persecute us. God calls us to treat with dignity, respect, and loving actions those who disagree with us, who worship differently than us, who follow a different God than us, who salute a different flag than us, who kneel during our national anthem, who aggressively try to destroy us, and those who we just generally find obnoxious! Those are hard words to hear—even harder to follow!

I've shared with you that my old tribe was big on literalism and inerrancy. It's amusing to hear how that group argues that Jesus didn't mean any of these things. Literalists celebrate Biblical inerrancy until they actually read the Bible. All too often, literalists want to disregard these very verses that we should accept at face value—if we're following Jesus.

The problem is that we can't follow them. It is simply not in us to live this way. Left to ourselves, we will hoard our goods, and fight violently against any that oppose us. Jesus describes a way of living that is humanly impossible—unless we ask for help! Only with the indwelling presence of the Holy Spirit will we find the strength to live this life. Even still, we'll spend our lifetimes learning to love like Jesus!

And, we will continue to fail—daily! But, we'll be in company with folks like the Apostle Paul, the chief of sinners, who knew the right thing to do but often did the wrong thing, anyway (Romans 7:14-25). We will try, and we will fall.

When we fall, we'll fall on grace. Discipleship reminds me of a toddler learning to walk. She takes a hesitant step or two and falls on her bottom. Never have I seen a good parent scold or punish that toddler for falling. Toddlers fall when they're learning to walk. It goes with the territory. A good parent picks the little girl up, dusts her off, consoles her, encourages her, and helps her try again, and again, and again, for as many times as it takes for her to walk freely. God is that kind of parent, never surprised when we fall. God knows who we are, knows falling goes with the territory. When we fall, God picks us up, dusts us off, consoles us, encourages us, and helps us try again, and again, and again for as long as it takes.

Let's not give up. Let's dare to fall as many times as it takes to get it right. Let's not settle for cheap grace. Let's allow this journey to be as difficult as it's supposed to be.

Let's continue to fail forward until, by God's grace, we get it right!

#7: We Water Down the Gospel When We Exclude People

Mark 2:13-17

13 Jesus went out again beside the sea; the whole crowd gathered around him, and he taught them. 14 As he was walking along, he saw Levi son of Alphaeus sitting at the tax booth, and he said to him, "Follow me." And he got up and followed him. 15 And as he sat at dinner in Levi's house, many tax collectors and sinners were also sitting with Jesus and his disciples—for there were many who followed him. 16 When the scribes of the Pharisees saw that he was eating with sinners and tax collectors, they said to his disciples, "Why does he eat with tax collectors and sinners?" 17 When Jesus heard this, he said to them, "Those who are well have no need of a physician, but those who are sick; I have come to call not the righteous but sinners."

Prayer

Lord, forgive us for dividing ourselves as insiders and outsiders. Give us the humility to recognize that none of us are worthy. Still, you came as the friend of sinners. Help us to welcome your divine friendship and to offer it to others, all others. Amen.

Jesus didn't come to invite us into an institution. Our call is not to be a part of an organization. No! God invites us to a Divine Romance! That image is far too often lost on those of us who have grown up in the western world. Generally, when I've heard people attempt to describe the Holy Trinity, they resort to some sort of diagram, like a triangle.

Father

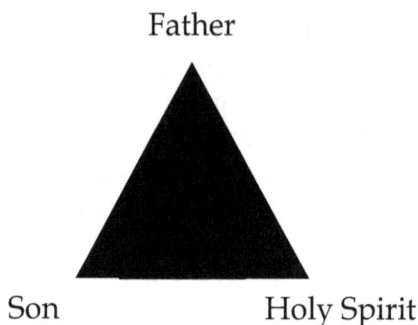

Son   Holy Spirit

In our American way of thinking about God, we divide the trinity into the same kind of structure we use with businesses. If God exists in three Persons, they must be CEO, CFO, and COO. We've unfortunately reduced the Holy Trinity into a divine board meeting. If you've sat through many board meetings, you might consider a divine board meeting an oxymoron.

We've lost sight of the beauty of the Divine Romance described by scripture and by some of the early saints of the church. When Cyril of Alexandria (412-444) considered the Trinity, he used the word *perichoresis*. The prefix *peri* means around as in the word perimeter. *Choresis* comes from the Greek *chorein* meaning to give way or make room. Together, they suggest the idea that each person of the Trinity moves around, making room for, even giving preference for one another. Some refer to this divine relationship as the Circle Dance, which is a beautiful metaphor for God and represents God much more faithfully than the more common institutional triangle.

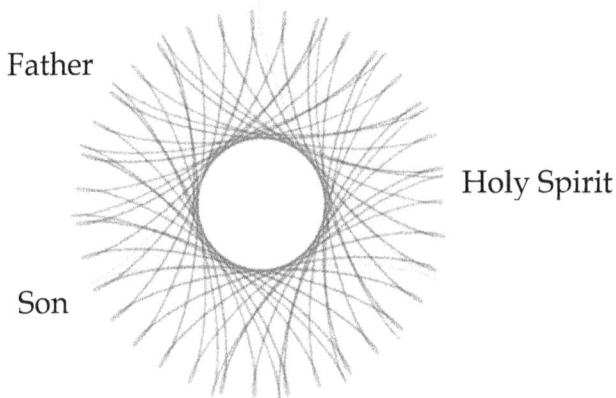

Father

Holy Spirit

Son

Not only is *perichoresis* a beautiful image, it's also a faithful representation of what we know of God through scripture. Father, Son, and Holy Spirit are all co-eternal. For all of eternity past, they've lived in loving relationship with one another, enjoying one another's company, giving preference to one another, glorifying one another. Their loving dance extends forward through eternity. The following passage from the Gospel of John, chapter five illustrates the relationships between Father and Son.

> 19 Jesus said to them, "Very truly, I tell you, the Son can do nothing on his own, but only

what he sees the Father doing; for whatever the Father does, the Son does likewise. 20 The Father loves the Son and shows him all that he himself is doing; and he will show him greater works than these, so that you will be astonished. 21 Indeed, just as the Father raises the dead and gives them life, so also the Son gives life to whomever he wishes. 22 The Father judges no one but has given all judgment to the Son, 23 so that all may honor the Son just as they honor the Father. Anyone who does not honor the Son does not honor the Father who sent him.

In these verses, we see the complete mutuality of love and respect. There's no competition between them, only mutual admiration. Later in the Gospel of John, Jesus explains the role of the Holy Spirit in *perichoresis*.

13 When the Spirit of truth comes, he will guide you into all the truth; for he will not speak on his own, but will speak whatever he hears, and he will declare to you the things that are to come. 14 He will glorify me, because he will take what is mine and declare it to you. 15 All that the Father has is mine. For this reason, I said that he will take what is mine and declare it to you. (John 16)

Again, this passage highlights the harmony that exists in the Holy Trinity. The dance began before the foundations of the world. It continues to this day and will continue throughout eternity. What a beautiful, comforting, inspiring view of God!

The most amazing of all miracles is that God invited us to join the dance! Christ looks at us, with all of our faults and failures. God knows all the times that we have failed to love God and others. In spite of all that I've done and left undone, God invites a scoundrel like me to dance! It really is amazing grace that God would include me in the Trinity. Jesus takes me by the hand and leads me into the same love, joy, and peace that defines God. The word that describes our participation in the Divine Dance is *theosis* which refers to union with God. The more we are perfected in love, the more united with the Trinity we are.

Even more amazing than my invitation to the dance is that Christ allows us to invite others. The disciple Andrew gives an obvious example. Upon meeting Jesus, his immediate response was to find his brother Simon (Peter) and invite him to Jesus. Like Andrew, God allows us to share with our friends and family the incredible message, "You won't believe who I've found! Come, join in the Divine Dance!" The story truly is remarkable! I love the thought of my loved ones and me forever embraced in the arms of God as we dance through eternity. It's great news!

But, then Jesus messes everything up! He invites someone else to the dance, someone that's not on *our* guest list. Someone with whom we would never attend a party. It doesn't take long for us to discover that Jesus' taste in dance partners is radically different from ours. That lesson was on full display for the scribes in this sermon text. After teaching a crowd of people, Jesus encounters Levi, also known as Matthew, sitting at his tax collector's booth. Levi was a thief and a traitor. As a tax collector, he worked for the occupying government of Rome, Israel's harsh enemy. Most First Century Jews had witnessed the violence of the *Pax Romana* (the peace of Rome). Most had lost a loved one to the cruel occupying forces, and Levi was working for them—traitor!

Additionally, tax collectors were allowed to collect and keep as much extra money as they could. After securing all that was due to Rome, they would shake down their fellow Jews for extra money to line their own pockets. No self-respecting Jew would invite Levi to a party, but Jesus says to him, "Follow me." Even worse, Jesus spends the afternoon partying at Levi's house with lots of other "undesirables," and the religious leaders notice. "Why does He eat with tax collectors and sinners?"

The disciples might have wondered about Jesus' odd guest list, too. It was an unlikely bunch. We've just met Levi, the traitor who worked for Rome. Also among the disciples was Simon the Zealot. Zealots worked for the violent overthrow of Rome. We would call him a terrorist. I wonder how many fights the disciples had to break up between the two of them. Jesus included on His team people who would never associate with one another and in some cases absolutely hated one another. He called them all friends.

Jesus does the same thing to us! While we're enjoying the beauty and serenity of the Circle Dance, He goes and invites more dance partners, people we can't stand. Maybe we don't think *those people* belong. Maybe we'd exclude them because of who they love, or the color of their skin, or the way they worship. Maybe they're here illegally. Maybe they wear a headdress we find offensive. They might not even speak English! We water down the gospel when we exclude people.

We also ruin the party for ourselves. Do you remember the story of the "Prodigal Son?" The ungrateful younger brother asks for his inheritance early and squanders it on wild living. Eventually, broke and defeated, he returns to his father's house to beg for a job. The father welcomes him warmly, cleans him up, dresses him in fine robes, and throws a party for him. The older brother, who's been so faithful, doesn't think his younger brother deserves a party and complains about it to their father. His dad encourages him to join in the festivities. In his own self-righteousness, he refuses and excludes himself from the party. If we reject those whom Christ invites, we may find that we have cut ourselves out of the celebration!

The kingdom of God is a party! It's God's party. God's the host. The kingdom is an eternal Circle Dance, and God has the lead. It is the Trinity's party, and God alone is in charge of the guest lists. We don't get a vote, regardless of how we feel about it.

I've occasionally shown up at parties only to find that the host invited someone I didn't like, someone with whom I try not to associate. On those occasions, I have to remind myself that it's not my party. Even if I don't like someone, I will treat that person with dignity and respect if for no other reason than to honor the host. If I truly love the host, I won't cause a problem at her party. I will treat people well for her sake! To do otherwise would ruin the party for me and damage my relationships with the host. I can make a scene, or I can enjoy the dance. I'm trying to learn to do the latter.

Those of us in the church must learn the same lesson. Christ controls the guest list. If we don't approve of someone on His dance card, it's our problem, not His. He clearly calls us to love the other people at the party. To do any less is to dishonor

Christ. If we claim to love Christ, we must choose to love all of those whom Christ loves.

We water down the Gospel when we exclude people from the dance.

In New Testament times, the Jews didn't think Gentiles belonged in the dance. God invited us anyway!

During the Protestant Reformation, Roman Catholics didn't think that Protestants belonged in the dance. God invited us anyway!

Much of the white church in American didn't think that African-Americans belonged in the dance. God invites them anyway!

Too many Christians still exclude people with tattoos, piercings, pink hair, and our LGBTQIA+ siblings from the dance. God keeps inviting!

In Acts 10, through a series of visions, God calls Peter to share the Gospel with a Gentile named Cornelius. Peter objects at first, based on his religion, based on his understanding of God. Peter resists God's call because he wants to be faithful to *his understanding* of God! God's response to Peter, "What God has called clean, you must not call profane" (Acts 10:15b). Peter makes the visit and shares the Gospel. Peter and his companions are shocked when they see the gift of the Holy Spirit given to Gentiles. Peter didn't particularly like God's dance card. God invited anyway. Later, in Acts 15, Peter pleads the Gentiles' case to the Jewish leadership of the church with a probing question, "If God has accepted them as they are, who are we to expect anything more?" (my paraphrase, cf. Acts 15:6-11). It's a question I ask myself frequently. I'm beginning to learn that my opinion doesn't really matter!

I do understand the discomfort of the Pharisees in the text! I've been one of them for too much of my life. I've excluded people because I didn't like their behavior. My critics called me "holier-than-thou," and they were right. I know too well what it's like to not be able to see past my own prejudices. I'm done with that! I'm through trying to dictate everyone's behavior. I'm tired of trying to identify the insiders and the outsider. I'd rather spend my time following Jesus, the Friend of sinners.

Together, let's invite the world to the Divine Dance!

#6: We Water Down the Gospel When We Tell People It's Clear and Simple

Matthew 22:36-40
36 "Teacher, which commandment in the law is the greatest?" 37 He said to him, "'You shall love the Lord your God with all your heart, and with all your soul, and with all your mind.' 38 This is the greatest and first commandment. 39 And a second is like it: 'You shall love your neighbor as yourself.' 40 On these two commandments hang all the law and the prophets."

Prayer
God of the universe, forgive our arrogance in believing we could define you. Open our eyes to see that you are unsearchable. Help us to embrace the mystery of who you are rather than suffer the limitation of what we think we know. Amen.

You could sum up my early Biblical interpretation with a bumper sticker I saw as a child, "God said it. I believe it. That settles it." That saying made perfect sense to me. It seemed clear cut. It emphasized the authority of scripture. It convinced me that the Bible had an answer for every question. In my college years, that simple phrase became even more straight-forward. In a sermon, one of my preachers asserted that we should take the middle sentence out of that bumper sticker. "God said it. That settles it!" My preacher explained that what we believe doesn't affect the truth at all. I carried this simplistic view of scripture through my college years and right into my early days in the pulpit.

As a self-proclaimed Bible scholar, I regularly used my bumper sticker hermeneutic to answer any question or solve any problem. It provided a simple formula to follow without much study and virtually no reason. Whenever I had a question or wanted to know the truth about any hot topic, I simply pulled out my concordance, searched for words associated with my topic, read the verses, and *voila'* I had the authoritative, God-breathed, answer. To improve my studies, while I was in seminary, I bought a *Strong's Exhaustive Concordance*, a book that lists every word in the Bible in alphabetical order and the verses in which that word is used. I could have saved some money by buying the abridged version that left out words like *a*, *an*, and *the*, but no price is too high when it comes to Biblical authority.

Of course, an even easier and much more common approach to Biblical authority is to not bother reading it. Let the preacher tell you what it says. As a preacher, I'm begging you: Do not take our word for it! Every preacher I've ever known is human, and all of us make mistakes. Please don't outsource your Bible study to the clergy. We're here to help, not do the job for you!

I'm one of those preachers who's made mistakes, and it's time to come clean. I cheated. Sometimes, when I began working my way through my concordance, using it as an answer key, I found verses I didn't like. The Bible offered some "answers" that didn't fit my beliefs. When confronted with those conflicts, I conveniently ignored those verses and kept searching until I found a better option. Even as a fundamentalist, I knew that the Bible isn't always so clear, but I would never admit it.

We water down the Gospel when we claim it's clear and simple. Let's look at some examples. Several months ago, a Facebook friend announced that she had found God's definitive answer about transsexuals. In her post was a picture of a Bible opened to Deuteronomy 22 with a red circle drawn around verse 5. "A woman shall not wear a man's apparel, nor shall a man put on a woman's garment; for whoever does such things is abhorrent to the Lord your God." King James calls it an abomination! For my Facebook friend, the answer was clear and simple. God said it. That settles it. (A perfect example of my youthful hermeneutic.) According to this literalist interpretation, it's an abomination for a man to wear woman's clothes or for a woman to wear man's clothes. Simple! Right? Or, is it? I happen to know that my Facebook friend considers herself a devout Christian, and I've frequently seen her wearing pants, for centuries considered men's clothing. Many devout women wear pants, football jerseys, and a variety of other clothes the author of Deuteronomy could never have considered. Additionally, when those words were first written, men wore ankle length robes that more closely resemble what we call dresses. It seems that my Facebook friend is offended by the notion of a man wearing a dress. She searched the scriptures, maybe with a concordance, until she found "proof" that God shares her prejudice. She used scripture to justify hatred. That's how simple it is to misuse the Bible.

Using scripture faithfully is rarely as clear and simple, as these other Biblical fashion statements illustrate.

- Leviticus 19:19—"You shall keep my statutes. You shall not let your animals breed with a different kind; you shall not sow your field with two kinds of seed; nor shall you put on a garment made of two different materials." No more polyester cotton blends! The Bible says so!
- Leviticus 19:27—"You shall not round off the hair on your temples or mar the edges of your beard." No more shaving for me! I could get behind this one.
- I Timothy 2:9—"Also that the women should dress themselves modestly and decently in suitable clothing, not with their hair braided, or with gold, pearls, or expensive clothes." For those who think they can ignore the previous verses because they're in the Old Testament, Paul weighs in with his own fashion advice to Timothy in the New Testament.

The Bible plainly says all of these things. We just don't believe them. If we define Biblical authority in terms of literalism and inerrancy, these verses pose a major problem unless we're prepared to radically alter our wardrobes.

Let me continue. It's not just our clothing that's under attack. It's our diet as well. Warning! This part gets painful! At least once every six weeks, my church gathers in our fellowship hall to participate in a public abomination. We come together as a church family to eat catfish, completely ignoring the authority of the Word of God. Leviticus 11:10 says, "But anything in the seas or the streams that *does not have fins and scales*, of the swarming creatures in the waters and among all the other living creatures that are in the waters—they are detestable to you" (emphasis added). I've preached way too many sermons about homosexuality, but not once have I threatened a Southerner's catfish! And, it gets worse. Forbidden by the same verse are shrimp, scallops, and oysters! I've been in the church for almost 55 years, and I've known hundreds of God-loving Christians. Not one of them has abstained from the seafood bar on religious principles. The Bible clearly says it. We clearly don't believe it.

Some Christians believe they've found their way around such odd prohibitions. "Those are Old Testament laws," they say, "I'm a New Testament Christian, and God abolished dietary laws in Acts 10." It's an argument worth pursuing. All of the dietary laws that I've mentioned are a part of the Law of Moses in the Old Testament. In Acts 10, God shows the Apostle Peter a vision of a tablecloth coming down from heaven filled with unclean foods, and Peter hears a voice from heaven, "Arise and eat all that's been blessed." Peter initially objects, but God convinces him not to call unclean what God has blessed. If that passage were the last one to mention dietary law, we could consider those laws as outdated, but the Bible says more. Five chapters later in Acts,

when the church is deciding whether to include
Gentiles, it makes this decision.

> "19 Therefore I have reached the decision that
> we should not trouble those Gentiles who are
> turning to God, 20 but we should write to
> them to abstain only from things polluted by
> idols and from fornication and from *whatever
> has been strangled* and *from blood* (emphasis
> added).

The final word on diet in the New Testament is that
meat must not be strangled nor eaten with the blood
still in it. Fried chicken from our church socials better
not come from birds that had their necks wrung! And,
I don't know any pastors who are prepared to preach
on the abomination of medium-rare steaks, either.
God said it, but if you look at the behavior of devout
Christ followers, it's definitely not settled.

Fundamentalists clamoring to protect their
literalist idea of Biblical authority argue that the
points I've made deal with ceremonial law and
dietary law. For them, those laws were abolished by
the cross. They argue that it's the moral law that
counts for Christians. Let's consider their argument
on two points. First, no First Century Jew would have
distinguished between moral, dietary, and ceremonial
law. Those are false divisions created much later by
people wrestling with the same issues we are. For
Jews in Jesus' day, there was only the Law. It was a
unified piece of work, inseparable. We can even see
this idea in the book of James in the New Testament.
"For whoever keeps the whole law but fails in one
point has become accountable for all of it" (2:10).
James was likely written in the First Century when
Christianity was largely a Jewish movement, and it
was possibly written before the fall of Jerusalem in C.

E. 72. We see in this one verse a unified view of the whole law that simply doesn't allow for our artificial separation into moral, ceremonial, and dietary. Secondly, if the moral law is all that matters for New Testament Christians, it's no less problematic. Let's look at some of the moral law which, according to fundamentalists, still defines our behavior.

The most frequent "moral law" debate of our time surrounds human sexuality, and the literalists argue that the answer is clear and simple. Our first example addresses the current litmus test for Biblical authority—homosexuality.

- Leviticus 20:13—"If a man lies with a male as with a woman, both of them have committed an abomination; they shall be put to death; their blood is upon them." This verse is from the Old Testament, but it's from the moral law, which, according to literalists, still applies. To be fair, I know many devout Christians who believe the first half of the verse, that homosexuality is an abomination. I used to be one of those. I know no devout Christians who believe the second part of the verse, "they shall be put to death." I never even went that far! Christians simply don't believe that we should run around executing homosexuals. We know better than to believe that part of the verse. We ignore that part of the "moral law" just like we do many other parts.
- Deuteronomy 25:5—"When brothers reside together, and one of them dies and has no son, the wife of the deceased shall not be married outside the family to a stranger. Her husband's brother shall go in to her, taking her in

marriage, and performing the duty of a husband's brother to her." If a man's brother dies, he is morally responsible to marry his sister-in-law and give her a son. The Bible says so. We don't believe it.

- Ephesians 5:5 says that greedy people don't have an inheritance in Christ, but our church culture celebrates greed. We evaluate pastoral success on the sizes of our staffs, our congregations, our buildings, our parsonages, and our salaries! We never preach against greed!
- Deuteronomy 23:1—"No one whose testicles are crushed or whose penis is cut off shall be admitted to the assembly of the Lord." I've had testicular cancer. The Bible says I'm cut off from the assembly of the Lord—no more church for me! It's clear and simple!
- I Corinthians 6:7 prohibits Christians from filing lawsuits. Go fire your lawyer. The Bible says so.
- Leviticus 20:9—"All who curse father or mother shall be put to death; having cursed father or mother, their blood is upon them." We don't believe that verse!

No one argues that Christian should follow these verses. In fact, there are very sound Biblical reasons for not following most of them.

What really amazes me is when literalists try to weasel out of verses that the Bible really expects us to follow. They have excuses for why we shouldn't do what Jesus expressly told us to do.

- Matthew 5:39—"But I say to you, 'Do not resist an evildoer. But if anyone strikes you on the right cheek, turn the other also'." Jesus gave that command to His followers (us), but I've heard dozens of excuses for why we shouldn't have to obey. (This verse has also been used to support abuse, especially spousal abuse. Nothing in Jesus' message should be construed to support any form of violence. These words are NOT telling you to just take it!)

- Matthew 5:40—"And if anyone wants to sue you and take your coat, give your cloak as well." Jesus tells us to let people take our stuff. The religious right in America almost unanimously opposes any kind of gun control. If you try to take a Christian's coat in my state, you're liable to get shot. That's not what Jesus said.
- Matthew 5:44—"But I say to you, 'Love your enemies and pray for those who persecute you'." Love for enemies is the singularly most defining characteristic of Christ-followers, but we find creative ways of excusing our hatred. One Christian actually responded to a blog about Jesus' words, "Sometimes the only way to love your enemies is to kill them."

We water down the Gospel when we tell people it's clear and simple! (I've included a list of Bible verses Christians don't believe at the end of this chapter.)

When I consider the list of prohibitions, I'm reminded that none of us is perfect, and I thank God for grace. The Law exists to prove that we need help. Christ provides the help regardless of what we've done.

If the Bible is not a clear and simple rulebook, then how do we use it? What is it good for? Is it useful at all?

The Bible is our most valuable tool for encountering Christ when we allow it to behave the way it was designed to behave. (Peter Enns has written several books that explore how the Bible is designed to behave. Check out *Revelation and Incarnation, The Bible Tells Me So, How the Bible Actually Works,* and *The Sin of Certainty*.) The Bible is not a rulebook, but a record of how hundreds of people have experienced God over a couple thousand years. Their experiences can lead us to our own God experiences. Following is a brief overview of a few guidelines. Each of them could be a chapter of this book by itself.

As I shared earlier, don't take the pastor's word for it. Check it out. Read the passages for yourself, including the ones I've shared. Check commentaries, Bible encyclopedias, and other study guides. People have been writing about scripture for centuries. Avail yourself of their knowledge.

Consider the context. Dr. Donald A. Carson, professor of New Testament at the Trinity Evangelical Divinity School, argues, "A text without a context is a pretext for a prooftext." In other words, interpreting scripture without any understanding of context will increase the likelihood of misinterpretation. Context includes the author, the original audience, and the culture in which the story was told or written. A passage written during the reign of King David when Israel was a superpower will likely reveal God differently than a passage written while the Jews are in exile in Babylon. The former will highlight how God gave them the victory.

The latter will question God's absence during a time of trial. Which is correct? That's the wrong question! Both share authentic experiences of God. Each one will speak to our lives differently during our variety of experiences. Both are true, if we don't treat them like an owner's manual.

Also, consider the writing style. Is it poetry, prophesy, or a letter? Literature style communicates meaning as well as the words themselves. If it's poetry, expect metaphors. If it's prophesy, the words were intended as instructions for a certain people in a certain time. Most of the New Testament consists of letters. The recipient of the letter tells us something about the message. Imagine that I have two children; the first is a workaholic, and the second is lazy. Now, imagine I'm writing letters to each. To the former I write, "You need to slow down. There's more to life than work. Enjoy!" And, I write to the second child, "You need to develop some drive. Work harder. Nothing worthwhile ever comes easy." Now, imagine I accidentally put each letter in the wrong envelope sending each sibling's letter to the other. Everything I wrote is true, but only if it gets to the right recipient. If the workaholic opens the letter telling him to work harder, I have misled him! What we know about the Bible will help us to hear what the Bible really says.

The Bible isn't super clear about much! I pray that my words encourage you to dig in and explore all that God says. I hope you'll move past a rulebook view of scripture and discover richness of relationship it invites. I admit, I'm not always sure how to navigate through all of its parts, and that's okay. It's okay to wrestle with the Bible. The Biblical authors did!

Here's what I do understand from the Bible. God calls us to love God and love others, all others. I pray that we will always read the scriptures through that lens.

20 Bible Verses Christians Don't Believe

1. Deuteronomy 22:5 A woman must not wear men's clothing, nor a man wear women's clothing, for the Lord your God detests anyone who does this. (No pants for women)

2. Leviticus 19:19 Keep my decrees. Do not mate different kinds of animals. Do not plant your field with two kinds of seed. Do not wear clothing woven of two kinds of material.

3. Leviticus 19:27 Do not cut the hair at the sides of your head or clip off the edges of your beard.

4. I Timothy 2:9 I also want the women to dress modestly, with decency and propriety, adorning themselves, not with elaborate hairstyles or gold or pearls or expensive clothes.

5. Leviticus 10:10 But all creatures in the seas or streams that do not have fins and scales—whether among all the swarming things or among all the other living creatures in the water—you are to regard as unclean. (What? No catfish? No shrimp? No Oysters?)

6. Acts 15:29 You are to abstain from food sacrificed to idols, from blood, from the meat of strangled animals and from sexual immorality. You will do well to avoid these things.

7. Leviticus 20:13 If a man has sexual relations with a man as one does with a woman, both of them have done what is detestable. They are to be put to death; their blood will be on their own heads.

8. Deuteronomy 25:5 If brothers are living together and one of them dies without a son, his widow must not marry outside the family. Her husband's brother

shall take her and marry her and fulfill the duty of a brother-in-law to her.

9. Ephesians 5:5 For of this you can be sure: No immoral, impure or greedy person—such a person is an idolater—has any inheritance in the kingdom of Christ and of God.

10. Deuteronomy 23:1 No one who has been emasculated by crushing or cutting may enter the assembly of the Lord. (No testicular cancer survivors).

11. I Corinthians 6:7 The very fact that you have lawsuits among you means you have been completely defeated already. Why not rather be wronged? Why not rather be cheated?

12. I Corinthians 14:34 Women should remain silent in the churches. They are not allowed to speak, but must be in submission, as the law says.

13. I Corinthians 11:5 But every woman who prays or prophesies with her head uncovered dishonors her head—it is the same as having her head shaved.

14. Romans 1:29 They have become filled with every kind of wickedness, evil, greed and depravity. They are full of envy, murder, strife, deceit and malice. They are gossips... (Gossips???)

15. Matthew 5:32 But I tell you that anyone who divorces his wife, except for sexual immorality, makes her the victim of adultery, and anyone who marries a divorced woman commits adultery.

16. Exodus 21: Rules on "proper" treatment of slaves.

17. Leviticus 20:9 Anyone who curses their father or mother is to be put to death. Because they have cursed their father or mother, their blood will be on their own head.

The Next Three We Should Believe But Often Resist

18. Matthew 5:39 But I tell you, do not resist an evil person. If anyone slaps you on the right cheek, turn to them the other cheek also.

19. Matthew 5:40 And if anyone wants to sue you and take your shirt, hand over your coat as well.

20. Matthew 5:44 But I tell you, love your enemies and pray for those who persecute you, 45 that you may be children of your Father in heaven.

#5 We Water Down the Gospel
When We Eliminate the Centrality
Of Social Justice

Micah 6:6-8

"With what shall I come before the Lord,
  and bow myself before God on high?
Shall I come before him with burnt offerings,
  with calves a year old?
Will the Lord be pleased with thousands of rams,
  with ten thousands of rivers of oil?
Shall I give my firstborn for my transgression,
  the fruit of my body for the sin of my soul?"
He has told you, O mortal, what is good;
  and what does the Lord require of you
but to do justice, and to love kindness,
  and to walk humbly with your God?

Prayer

Lord, sometimes we are so careful about the appearance of following you. We refrain from foul language. We show up for church. We listen to Christian music and wear Christian t-shirts. We want the world to see us as believers, but we have too often neglected the more important things of the law:

justice, mercy, and faithfulness. Teach us to follow you by the way that we love and serve others. Amen.

The principle of social justice makes a lot of American church goers squirm. The Biblical call to justice, mercy, and faithfulness makes us nervous. It's just not the American way! I'm reminded on the beer commercial from my childhood. "You only go around once in life, so you better grab all the gusto you can get." That commercial sounds more like our culture. "Grab all you can. Clench it with an iron fist, or somebody will take it away from you." We've decorated our worship spaces with the Stars and Stripes while Christians join the chorus of "America First!" Social justice is a threat. It'll take some of what I have and give it to someone who didn't work for it. It'll take American resources and "waste" them on people who don't deserve them.

Some will consider my words hyperbole. They'll argue that we support homeless shelters and food pantries. We pay utilities and help with rent. Some of our churches do enough to assuage our guilt, but it's simply not enough when millions die each day of hunger and hunger related diseases. We've made ourselves feel better, but we have solved very few problems.

Other churches have given up the fight all together—as a manner of principle. Those churches loudly assert that Christianity is all about being born again. For them, it's personal commitment between the individual and Christ. They call for repentance of *individual* sins like cussing and drinking and looking at inappropriate things on the internet, and they demand that the individual clean up his or her act. (Stop doing those things you repented of.) Mention social justice in those churches, and they'll accuse you of watering down the Gospel!

It happened to me at a church I served years ago. Our leadership team was working to define the core values for our ministry. We were putting in writing the central principles and beliefs that would govern our behavior. Things like Biblical authority passed unanimously without discussion. The debate began in earnest when we introduced the subject of social justice. The proposed core value read, "All our ministries will promote social justice and evangelism." Some of our leaders quickly balked at the social justice part. They refused to consider this statement as a core value unless we qualified what we meant by social justice. After much discussion, those leaders agreed to the value provided that we define (and limit) social justice to the things outlined in Matthew 25: feeding the hungry, clothing the naked, providing shelter to the homeless, and water for the thirsty. They wouldn't have us getting too carried away with justice and mercy. To this day, I wonder about the cause of their fear!

Earlier still in my ministry, a small church invited me to come offer a consultation for their ministry. Their average worship attendance was about 50. They were mostly retired, and they were wisely concerned about the future of their church. In preparation for the meeting, I obtained demographic information on the community in which the church was located. I discovered a high density of young families and a very high density of single mothers. Nothing about the membership of the church resembled its community. Immediately, some obvious strategies came to mind. I discussed with the church the possibility of offering a Mom's Morning Out, after school care, or tutoring. Obviously, reaching their community required meeting people at their point of need. I was young enough and naïve enough to believe that I had solved their problems. As we discussed the possibilities of these outreach activities, one woman in the church spoke up, "Well, this just sounds to me like Social Gospel." Her statement ended the meeting. Apparently, she wielded considerable influence in the church. When she labeled my outreach ideas as Social Gospel, it was the death knell for my consultation, and eventually for that congregation. They continued to believe their community just needed to get saved. They rejected the idea of offering justice ministries to their community. It was only a matter of a few years until the church doors closed for good. That church, and many like it, would sooner die than devote themselves to social justice!

As critical as I may sound, I must say that I do understand the sentiment. From my early years, I was taught the dangers of the Social Gospel movement. That movement, I was told, only cared about feeding people and housing people and teaching people, but they didn't care about people being born again. They asked questions like, "What good is it to feed and clothe someone if they're going to end up in hell, anyway?" For years, I bought into their logic. I fought against that watered-down Social Gospel in favor of a more Biblical Christianity.

For all those years, I was blind to the centrality of social justice in the scriptures. I blatantly ignored what the Bibles says about justice and mercy while clinging to an illusion of a Bible-centered faith. Once I truly began to listen to the scripture, I discovered a shocking truth. **We water down the**

Gospel when we eliminate the centrality of social justice!

Justice and mercy are two of the most recurring themes throughout the Bible. For 400 years, the Israelites were slaves in Egypt. After freeing them, God continually reminds them of their years in Egypt with dozens of instructions to never treat anyone as the Egyptians treated them. "Don't forget your years in slavery. Let that experience remind you to treat people right." The entire tone of scripture, from cover to cover, is to treat people better than you were treated.

Before Israel could even reach the Promised Land, God began instructing them on justice. "When you reap the harvest of your land, you shall not reap to the very edges of your field, or gather the gleanings of your harvest; you shall leave them for the poor and for the alien: I am the Lord your God" (Leviticus 23:22). God gave a simple and beautiful image of social justice. When you do the hard work of planting, when you invest your seed, when you labor in your fields, *don't gather the full fruit of your labor.* Don't reap the edges that *you* planted. Leave them for people you don't know, for the homeless, and for the immigrant! How un-American! I've lived in places where you could get shot for gathering food from someone else's field! It's no wonder these passages make us nervous. Yet, God wrote into Israel's constitution that those who have resources will freely share with those who don't! We water down the Gospel when we ignore those numerous passages.

A similar passage carries the same message. "You shall not strip your vineyard bare, or gather the fallen grapes of your vineyard; you shall leave them for the poor and the alien: I am the Lord your God"

(Leviticus 19:10). God's expectation is that God's people will be generous with what God has provided. When we ignore social justice, we act as though we deserve all that we own. Scripture teaches us that everything we have is a gift from God. It all belongs to God who clearly says to give away some to provide for the immigrant!

Again, borne out of a heritage of slavery, God demands justice for strangers. "You shall not oppress a resident alien; you know the heart of an alien, for you were aliens in the land of Egypt" (Exodus 23:9). Immigrants are even welcomed into the holiest of meals in Judaism, the Passover. These passages remind us that just as God has been generous with us who do not deserve it, we should be even more generous with others, even when we think they don't deserve it.

Perhaps the greatest Old Testament symbol of social justice is the Year of Jubilee. God instructed the Israelites to set aside every 50th year as a jubilee. In that year, all slaves would be freed, all debts would be forgiven, and all land would revert to its original owners. Twice each century, the slate would be wiped clean, and families would get a fresh start. What a beautiful leveling of the playing field. Not surprisingly, I've never found evidence that Israel celebrated the Year of Jubilee even once. I suspect the reason for ignoring God's command is that it depends on the people in power surrendering that power to those who have been disenfranchised. Ignoring God's expressed commands, people in power clung to power. Some things haven't changed in the 4000 years since the Exodus.

Some will dismiss my examples as Old Testament Law, and therefore no longer applicable. It is odd, however, that New Testament Christians would reject portions of the Old Testament for being too merciful and too graceful, attributes we normally ascribe to the New Testament. So, in case there is any doubt about the validity of these Old Testament passages for Christians, let's look at Jesus' own mission statement. Jesus began His earthly ministry by claiming for Himself this quote from Isaiah.

"The Spirit of the Lord is upon me,
because he has anointed me
to bring good news to the poor.
He has sent me to proclaim release to the captives
and recovery of sight to the blind,
to let the oppressed go free,
to proclaim the year of the Lord's favor." (Luke 4:18-19)

As if to accentuate His position, Jesus stops His quote of the prophet in the middle of a sentence. The passage Jesus quotes in Isaiah continues, "and the day of vengeance of our God" (Isaiah 61:2b). Jesus embraced the social justice part of Isaiah's message while ignoring the vengeance part. He made social justice the cornerstone of His ministry. Regardless of our ideas about personal salvation and new birth, we water down the Gospel when we eliminate the centrality of social justice. Christ put it at the center of His ministry. Can we do any less?

Jesus asked for more than our agreement with a set of beliefs. The life He offers is not defined by the acceptance of certain tenets of faith. Rather than asking for belief, Jesus calls us to follow! Christians go where Jesus goes and do what Jesus does. People who follow Christ treat other people the way that Christ did in His earthly ministry. Christians' relationships are defined by love, mercy, forgiveness, and justice. Those characteristics describe Christ followers' relationships with friends and enemies, with the faithful and the faithless, with the seekers and the doubters. Jesus offered love, mercy, forgiveness, and justice to all. His followers must do the same.

What does following look like for us? What are the practical implications of following Christ in the 21st Century? For most of us, social holiness will require a radical shift in world view. We resist engaging in social justice, because we've convinced ourselves of the just order of society as it is. We imagine that whatever affluence we enjoy is well-deserved, a due profit for our hard work and good behavior. We did the work, stayed in school, paid the tuition, got the degree, and work the 50 and 60 hour weeks required to get us where we are, and we are not likely to share it. If we are doing well, it's well deserved.

Conversely, we tend to blame people for being poor. Since we are certain that our good behavior brought good things to us, we naturally assume that bad behavior must be the root cause of poverty, hunger, and homelessness. People must be in destitute situations, we assume, because they dropped out of school, or didn't work hard enough to make the grades, or started using drugs. Modern opinions of affluence and poverty are remarkably similar to the theology of the Pharisees who claimed that blessings are evidence of God's favor while sickness and poverty are judgement, God's judgement against sin.

Jesus vigorously opposed the theology of the Pharisees and calls us to be renewed by transforming our minds to His way of thinking. To follow Jesus, we must stop taking credit for our privilege. To be honest, much of that privilege is due to where we were born, the color of our skin, the makeup of our families, and cultural norms that happened to favor us. We can take credit for none of those conditions. Ultimately, every blessing we enjoy is a gift from God given with a purpose. Just as God blessed Abraham to be a blessing to the world, so God blesses us to be a blessing. If God has allowed an abundance in your life, hear it as God's calling for you to bless someone else with that gift. To act differently would align us with the villain in one of Jesus' parables in Luke 12.

> 16 Then he told them a parable: "The land of a rich man produced abundantly. 17 And he thought to himself, 'What should I do, for I have no place to store my crops?' 18 Then he said, 'I will do this: I will pull down my barns and build larger ones, and there I will store all my grain and my goods. 19 And I will say to my soul, Soul, you have ample goods laid up for many years; relax, eat, drink, be merry.' 20 But God said to him, 'You fool! This very night your life is being demanded of you. And the things you have prepared, whose will they be?' 21 So it is with those who store up treasures for themselves but are not rich toward God."

God was not angry with the man for his success, but for his greed. Upon receiving a blessing, the man chose to hoard rather than share. Jesus' parable is as challenging today as when He first told it.

Faithfully following Jesus requires that we stop blaming people for their difficult circumstances. Sure, they've made some bad choices. Haven't we all! Many of us survived those bad decisions while others did not. Because we've made our mistakes, God calls us to be gentle with others who make mistakes. It's healthy to address bad behavior and offer opportunities for growth. It is unacceptable to refuse help to people who have made mistakes because "They're getting what they deserve." The Pharisees blamed people. Jesus did not.

If we are serious about following Jesus, we must be willing to see the injustice baked into our culture. Americans feed more meat to our pets than people get to eat in the developing world. Awareness of the absurdity challenges us to wrestle with the difficulties that social justice presents. God invites us to do the hard work of discovering what real help looks like. Handing out $20 bills on the street corner could ease our guilt and give us a sense of altruism, but it probably doesn't help much and likely even hurts. Real help requires building relationships with people who are struggling and working with them to find solutions. It will cost more than our money. It'll cost our time!

Answers still elude me. Melissa and I love to cruise for our vacations. The chance to disconnect from daily life and explore the world is refreshing for our bodies, minds, and spirits. The cost of our vacations convicts me. Should I use that money to alleviate suffering in some part of the community? Why do I deserve to travel in luxury while others are homeless? Those are valid questions, but the answers aren't easy. When we cruise, we're helping to employ thousands of under-resourced crew members who are supporting families back home. Melissa and I have had numerous conversations with those men and women who can provide for their families for years with the salaries they'll make on an eight-month contract. If we stop cruising, we take money away from those hard-working, developing world citizens who are trying to make a better living. Maybe I'm just justifying our vacations. I share this example to suggest that the social justice demands of the Gospel are challenging. If we would follow Christ, we must at least be willing to wrestle with these questions.

"In Christ, God was reconciling the world to Himself" (II Corinthians 5:19a). Christ called us to join in that ministry of reconciliation. A life of reconciliation requires both recognizing the socio-economic gaps that divide people and taking strong actions to close those gaps. It's not a problem we'll solve with one worship service or one meeting, but we can start making a difference, today. If we are really following Christ, then today let's do something tangible to demonstrate the love of God to those who have been left out or left behind.

#4: We Water Down the Gospel When We Explain Away Nonviolent Love of Enemies

Matthew 5:43-48

43 "You have heard that it was said, 'You shall love your neighbor and hate your enemy.' 44 But I say to you, Love your enemies and pray for those who persecute you, 45 so that you may be children of your Father in heaven; for he makes his sun rise on the evil and on the good, and sends rain on the righteous and on the unrighteous. 46 For if you love those who love you, what reward do you have? Do not even the tax collectors do the same? 47 And if you greet only your brothers and sisters, what more are you doing than others? Do not even the Gentiles do the same? 48 Be perfect, therefore, as your heavenly Father is perfect.

Prayer

God of love, forgive us for the ways we attack one another. Forgive us for the walls we erect between your children. Help us, today, to discover more fully the depth of love you have for all of us created in your image. Empower us to follow Christ's commandment to love others as He has loved us. Amen.

It's at the heart of the Gospel, the very foundation of our beliefs—Love God, Love Others!

Those words occupy such a central place in Christianity that they're often called the Great Commandment. Jesus said that the entire Law is contained in His instruction to love God with all that we are and all that we have and to love our neighbors as ourselves. That kind of love was the defining characteristic of the early Christians. "See how they love one another," was the observation of First and Second Century pagans when they considered the Christians in their community.

It sounds wonderful! Who could argue with love? But, let's face it, there are some difficult people in the world!

- Those who cut us off in traffic, prompting the one-fingered wave,
- In-laws,
- Other races,
- Those who don't love like we think they should,
- People who hate us,
- People who want to kill us (whoever the current terrorist group is.)

When we consider those people, Jesus' words seem very hard, almost harsh. Am I really supposed to love *them*? Surely, Jesus wasn't talking about *those people* when He spoke those words.

Church folks work hard to avoid this commandment. A couple of years ago, I was in a denominational meeting where the discussion centered on how inclusive we would be of our LGBTQIA+ siblings. Before voting on any resolutions or petitions pertaining to the issue, we clergy and laity gathered in table discussions. One of the men at my table, a retired pastor, shared with a great bit of frustration, "All week they've just wanted to talk about love. We need to get down to what the Bible says." Blinded by the issue, my colleague failed to see that love is the heart of the Gospel.

Jesus makes it abundantly clear. If you only choose to love the people who love you in return, you've accomplished nothing. People who don't believe in God do that much. People who love Christ love their enemies! We water down the Gospel when we explain away nonviolent love of enemies. And, people who claim to be Biblical literalists will explain away these verses more than almost any others. They would never explain away verses about murder or adultery or theft. Upon catching a spouse in an affair, they never say, "That's not really what the Bible means." We don't make excuses for the people stealing our cars or shooting our neighbors. But, when it comes to loving our enemies, Bible believing Christians have created a long list of excuses. Dr. Benjamin Corey, whose blog *Formerly Fundie* inspired this sermon series, shared this list of real-life excuses from real-life church goers.

- I don't think the issue is as simple as you're making it.
- Are you sure that's what God actually said?
- I don't think nonviolence is what God actually meant. Sometimes loving a person means you have to kill them.
- When Paul forbids violence, I think he was speaking to a specific cultural issue.
- The nonviolence was just limited to some specific contexts.

- You can't accept "love your enemies" at face value. You need to consider the Old Testament, too.
- If you think loving enemies means you can't kill them, you're just showing your liberal bias.
- I don't care if the entire early church was against violence, that doesn't mean they were always right.
- There are plenty of exceptions to this rule. What if Hitler raped your wife?
- When Jesus said enemies, He didn't mean people who wanted to kill you. He was talking about difficult neighbors.
- There's no way Jesus could mean don't kill them. Jesus was the Old Testament God, and He killed babies back then.
- You would dishonor God if you didn't blow the head off of an intruder.
- It would not glorify God if you allowed yourself to be killed by an enemy.
- Jesus only lived nonviolence because He had to die, but that doesn't mean we need to do the same thing. He never intended for us to copy everything He did.
- You must be a Democrat, trying to twist scripture for your own political purposes.

Jesus' command to love our enemies can lead even the staunchest fundamentalist to whole-heartedly embrace "liberal" Biblical interpretation. These church goers readily ignored key themes in scripture to justify hatred. "It would not glorify God if you allowed yourself to be killed by an enemy." That one quote, if it were true, invalidates the very mission of

Christ, to allow Himself to be killed by His enemies in order to glorify God. That quote alone, underscores how far we Christians will go to protect our own self-interest and to justify our hatred of our enemies!

Matthew 5:43-48 summarizes Jesus' more explicit teachings about nonviolent enemy love earlier in the Sermon on the Mount. He felt so strongly about it that He overruled Old Testament law that obstructed His view of love for enemies in action, thoughts, and feelings.

Jesus quotes Exodus 21:24 "You have heard that it was said, 'An eye for an eye and a tooth for a tooth'" (Matthew 5:38). Jesus references the Law with which His audience was familiar. At the same time, He connects with our desire for revenge, but He supersedes both when He continues, "But I say to you, 'Do not resist an evildoer. But if anyone strikes you on the right cheek, turn the other also'" (Matthew 5:39). We Christians cling to our grudges. We hunger for revenge. We know Christ's command to forgive others, yet we resist to our own demise. Unforgiveness is like drinking poison and waiting for our enemies to die. We resist Jesus' command to love even if it kills us. During my 54 years in the church, I've heard countless explanations for why Jesus couldn't possibly mean what He says. None of those explanations holds water. Jesus initiated a new kingdom with a new law that leaves no room for revenge. We water down the Gospel when we explain away nonviolent enemy love.

It's not just hateful actions that concern Jesus but our words, too. In Matthew 5:22b, Jesus teaches that anyone who says, "You fool," will be in danger of the fires of hell. I struggle with that one because I can so easily be critical of others (as though I have it all figured out). While watching the news, I've frequently called certain politicians fools, or worse. I've blurted out unseemly epithets at other drivers in traffic. Refraining from hateful words is hard, but it's one of the strings attached to following Jesus. Ultimately, I try to remember that when we curse others, we curse Jesus. We water down the Gospel when we explain away nonviolent enemy love. Hateful, critical language is a part of me that has to die!

Jesus' desire for us to love extends from our actions, to our words, and even to our emotions. In Matthew 5:21-22, Jesus equates murder with anger. To harbor anger in our hearts toward another human made in God's image is on par with taking a life. (To be clear, anger and murder may be equivalent for the person who is angry, but not for person who is the object of that anger. I'd rather you be mad at me than kill me. Sin and its consequences are separate issues.) Jesus knows that whatever is in our hearts works its way into our words and actions. We water down the Gospel when we explain away nonviolent enemy love. Love must transform the heart!

I understand why people resist the command to love our enemies! It's hard. It's beyond us to love like Jesus tells us to love, but we must. It's those who love like Jesus who will be children of the Father. "But I say to you, 'Love your enemies and pray for those who persecute you, so that you may be children of your Father in heaven'" (Matthew 5:44-45a). That verse contains a clue to teach us how to love. All of us together, our friends and our enemies, are children of one Father! God loves us all, equally. Our hatred for one another does not evoke God's anger or wrath or vengeance. When we hate one another, it breaks

God's heart! I remember the day that my older two children got into a fist fight. They were legitimately angry with one another, and I found myself pulling them off each other trying to separate them. I didn't care who won (or was winning). I wasn't terribly concerned with what issue prompted the fight. I saw my children rolling in the parking lot, trying to hurt one another, and it devasted me. I wanted nothing more than peace for my children. God is a much more perfect Parent than I am, but I have to believe that when we fight, it breaks God's heart in ways we can't imagine. I'm certain that God desires our peace more than we can understand. If we truly love God, maybe we can learn to love one another if for no other reason than because of our love for God!

Still, we will have to love some people from a distance. Loving others doesn't always mean we can be together with them. We must learn to love toxic people without exposing ourselves to their poison. We can continue to love dangerous people with our thoughts, words, and actions without endangering ourselves.

Ultimately, if we want to love like Jesus, we'll need help! We can invite the Holy Spirit to help us to fall more and more deeply in love with God. The more we love God, the more able we are to see people as God sees them. When we see our enemies through God's eyes, we will love our enemies.

I invite you to respond to this message in two ways. First, fall in love with God, deeply. Make room in your daily schedule to listen to God and rest in God's presence. Second, ask God to help you love and pray for your enemies. God is always prepared to answer that prayer!

#3: We Water Down the Gospel
When We Overemphasize Rarely Mentioned Sins in Scripture

II Timothy 3:14-17
14 But as for you, continue in what you have learned and firmly believed, knowing from whom you learned it, 15 and how from childhood you have known the sacred writings that are able to instruct you for salvation through faith in Christ Jesus. 16 All scripture is inspired by God and is useful for teaching, for reproof, for correction, and for training in righteousness, 17 so that everyone who belongs to God may be proficient, equipped for every good work.

Prayer
Lord Jesus, in all our studies, remind us that you are the Word of God sent into the world to reconcile humanity to God. Forgive us for revering the Bible more than you. Teach us to use and share the scriptures in a loving way that connects people to God. Amen.

In Ephesians, Paul calls the Word of God the Sword of the Spirit. Later in his life, Paul wrote the above words to Timothy, reminding him that all scripture is inspired by God and useful for teaching, reproof, correction, and training. Before we dig into the authority of scripture for our lives, we should ask a few questions.

First, what does Paul mean by the phrase "Word of God?" For centuries, we've applied that term to the Holy Bible. I remember the days when it was common for church youth groups to have "sword drills," competitions to see which teen could find a particular Bible book, chapter, and verse the fastest. It's generally assumed in our culture that the Bible is the Word of God. The Bible itself calls that assumption into question. According to the Apostle John, "The Word became flesh and made his dwelling among us" (John 1:14a). For John, Jesus was the Word of God. So, is the Bible the word of God, or is Jesus? Which should have more authority in our lives?

Second, what does Paul include in his understanding of scripture when he writes to Timothy? Christians generally assume that Paul is referring to the 66 books of our Protestant Bibles, but that assumption causes several problems. When Paul wrote those words, the scriptures consisted of the Hebrew Bible, what we call the Old Testament, and there was still some disagreement about which books should be included in it. The New Testament wasn't canonized (officially authorized) until the Council of Carthage in 397 CE. Even today, the Bibles of the Protestants, Roman Catholics, and Orthodox churches each have different numbers of books. All this information begs the question, "Which scriptures are useful for teaching, reproof, correction, and training?"

For the purpose of this sermon, we'll assume that scripture refers to the 66 books of the Protestant Bible. Those books are an essential weapon for fighting evil—not each other. Far too often, Christians have used their knowledge of the Bible to attack those with whom they disagree, too frequently driving wedges between people and God.

Here's how we do it. Suppose I don't like tattoos. That's my opinion, and I'm welcomed to it. No one is forcing me to get one. But, if I can prove that the Bible agrees with me, then I can feel free to force my opinion on others. So, I scour the scriptures for evidence to support my bias. My concordance leads me to Leviticus 19:28 which says not to put tattoo marks on your body. That settles it. God agrees with me, and I can tell others not to get tattoos. If I'm in a position of authority, I can forbid them. I can use the Bible to turn my opinion into Law. Dangerous! Of course, if I had any integrity at all, I would have to follow everything included in that passage from Leviticus.

> 26 "'Do not eat any meat with the blood still in it. "'Do not practice divination or seek omens. 27 "'Do not cut the hair at the sides of your head or clip off the edges of your beard. 28 "'Do not cut your bodies for the dead or put tattoo marks on yourselves. I am the Lord.

If I am going to judge people for their tattoos, then I must also stop eating my medium rare steaks. (Never!) If I oppose ink, I must also oppose haircuts. (As I write these words, it's been about two months since my last haircut due to shelter in place orders for COVID-19. If haircuts are a sin, I will sin as soon as the barber shops open!) Leviticus 19:34 continues "The foreigner residing among you must be treated as your native-born. Love them as yourself, for you were foreigners in Egypt. I am the Lord your God." In many parts of the American church, you're much more likely to hear a sermon denouncing tattoos than you are to hear a sermon supporting immigrants! We've created an uncomfortable trap for ourselves by overemphasizing rarely mentioned sins in the Bible.

I am certainly guilty of majoring in the minors. I've preached against all sorts of rarely mentioned sins, especially those of which I'm not guilty.

From the pulpit, I've denounced people who read their horoscopes, go to palm readers, or play with Ouija boards. My text for those attacks was the Leviticus passage mentioned above that discourages use of mediums or spiritists. As long as I could avoid the daily horoscopes in the newspaper, I could feel superior to so many other people.

In the 1980s and 90s, I denounced rock music. Televangelists exposed rock bands for using "backwards masking" to communicate satanic message to unwitting teenagers. Supposedly, by playing albums backwards we would be influenced to revolt against God, stop going to church, and join a cult. For awhile I bought into their message. I didn't want to be tricked by the devil. I dutifully destroyed my collection: *Styx*, *The Eagles*, and *Chicago*—real dangerous stuff. Oddly, the Bible never even mentions rock music, but when I was so focused on weeding out every evil from every rarely mentioned sin, it was a short leap to include sins that are not even mentioned. (The only true pain rock music caused me is when I had to pay the price, years later, to replace my collection.)

I was equally opposed to Halloween, the devil's holiday. I preached against the celebration, forbade my kids from Trick-or-Treating, and generally felt superior to everyone who wore orange and black in October. Once, while serving as a youth director, the church's mid-week meal followed the Halloween theme. I walked out in protest. There was no way I would drink "witch's brew!" Again, I went to war over something on which scripture is completely silent. When we shine such a bright light on such small concerns, we actually give them greater power.

It's not just my immature, fundamentalist preaching. We've built entire institutions around rarely mentioned topics.

In some denominations, divorce *permanently* disqualifies a person from service. Repentance doesn't help. Even when one spouse deserts the other, the abandoned spouse can never serve in church leadership. This lifetime prohibition is based on six passages of scripture written centuries ago to very different cultures. At the time those prohibitions were written, women had no legal authority, and wives could be disposed of for any displeasure caused to their husbands, including burning dinner. Once divorced, a woman's prospects for survival likely depended on prostitution or begging. In that culture, scripture prohibits divorce, largely as a protection for women. While women are still not guaranteed equality in 21st Century America, their rights have improved greatly over the last 2000 years. Biblical prohibitions make perfect sense in context. Today's excessive punishments for divorce are not the result of reason but are evidence of overemphasizing rarely mentioned verses in the Bible.

Some Christian groups take a similarly strong stance against the consumption of alcohol. Their responses vary from frowning upon the practice to completely excluding those who drink. (I deal more extensively with this issue in my book, *The Immoral Christian*.) To be clear, the Bible does offer numerous cautions against overindulgence, but it also celebrates wine as a good thing. Rather than offering a "clear-cut, once and for all time rule," the Bible offers variety in its message. Paul cautions, "Do not get drunk with wine" (Ephesians 5:18). On the other hand, Jesus' first miracle was at a wedding that ran out of wine. After the guests had drunk freely, Jesus made 120-150 more gallons of wine. Too many Christians have made a doctrinal stand on an issue that is simply not central to scripture.

It's not surprising that a male-dominated religion highlights obscure Bible verses to limit and control the role of women in the church. In I Corinthians 14, Paul, speaking to a particular church in a particular situation, urges women to remain silent in church. Male leaders in a patriarchal religion seized on that verse to limit the influence of women. To achieve the marginalization of women, though, required those same male leaders to ignore other verses that claim there is no difference between male or female (Galatians 3:28), and they ignore the testimony of scripture regarding the role of women. In all four Gospels, the first people to announce the resurrection were women. They were the first evangelists! Early church leaders included the likes of Lydia, Priscilla, and Junia.

It's not enough to control female preaching and leadership. Some male church leaders appeal to obscure verses to control the way that women dress. They cite I Timothy 2:9 as an excuse to dictate women's clothing. It's true that Paul does say, "The women should dress themselves modestly and decently in suitable clothing, not with their hair braided, or with gold, pearls, or expensive clothes," but this verse has been wildly distorted to make women responsible for men's bad sexual behavior. (See *The Immoral Christian* for more on the church's abuse of this modesty verse.) Paul is not criticizing women for showing too much skin but for flaunting their wealth in front of the poor. Male dominated Christianity would rather attack women than deal honestly with our greed. We water down the Gospel when we emphasize obscure verses to further oppress marginalized people!

The entire Bible is useful for teaching and correcting ourselves. We should interpret these words of Paul to Timothy in light of the Sermon on the Mount. In Chapter Three, we reviewed Jesus' caution against trying to remove a speck from another's eye while we still have a plank in our own eyes. Rather than using rarely mentioned sins in the Bible to attack others, we should apply the lessons of scripture to our own lives, especially those lessons that are mentioned constantly in scripture. The rarely mentioned sins are important, but shouldn't we focus our attention on those things that the Bible mentions most often? When we focus on the rarely mentioned sins that others are doing, we get to water down our own disobedience.

The two most often mentioned sins in scripture get very little mention from our pulpits.

Very rarely are they the subject of Sunday school lessons. Innocence or repentance of these two sins is not a requirement for leadership or even ordination in most churches. American Christians are hardly concerned at all about the two things that the Bible says concern God the most!

Idolatry is one of those sins. It breaks God's heart and is the frequent cause of broken relationships with God throughout the pages of scripture. Many modern people think that we get a pass on this one because we don't bow down and worship little statues of false gods. We've mistakenly assumed that idolatry only means worshipping a golden calf or some other graven image. In reality, anything that takes God's place in our lives is an idol. Anything to which we give our primary devotion or that is our source of strength and inspiration can become an idol. Some people rely on money for security and happiness. For others, reputation or popularity is all that matters. Still, for others, the center of their lives is sports or possessions. I live in Tuscaloosa, Alabama. I'm a proud alumnus of the University of Alabama and a huge fan of Alabama athletics. On Saturdays in August and September, you'll likely find me in Bryant-Denny Stadium in 100-degree weather cheering on the Tide. Hundreds of us in that crowd regularly attend worship services in our local churches. Many of us will complain on Sunday morning if the temperature in the sanctuary gets over 72-degrees. How much we'll tolerate to participate in an activity reveals something of its importance. Idolatry is everywhere. I'm guilty! Most of us are! So, why do we ignore sins that the Bible obsesses over? Because we water down the Gospel! Because we'd rather use the Bible to attack others than to correct ourselves.

The other of the most often mentioned sins in the Bible is greed. Scripture is enormously preoccupied with greed while the American church rarely mentions it. To the contrary, greed is our metric for success for us clergy. "Faithfulness in ministry" is rewarded with bigger churches, bigger staffs, bigger salaries, and bigger parsonages. The American church has completely blended into the American culture of more, more, more. We'd rather preach against things that are counter-cultural, like tattoos, than become counter-cultural by repenting of our greed, surrendering all we have to the poor, and following Christ. This message is not the one I want to hear when I'm thinking about buying my next boat or planning my next extravagant vacation. So the church remains silent on this central tenet of scripture. We water down the Gospel when we overemphasize rarely mentioned sins in scripture while conveniently neglecting the ones that are talked about constantly.

What if we really applied God's word to our own lives for teaching, rebuking, encouraging, and training? What would it look like to put God ahead of our idols? What would it look like to share with those who have less? What would it be like to live in loving relationship with those whom we've marginalized?

While serving a previous church, I invited a discipleship group to serve a meal at the local homeless shelter. It was important to me that this service project be more than ministry *to* the homeless. It needed to be ministry *with* the homeless. I asked the group to provide the food and serve it to the residents of the shelter, but I also asked my group to fix their own plates and sit with the residents, to enjoy a meal together. In the days leading up to the event, several of my church members expressed concern, even fear, about eating with homeless people. Some of our members had been faithful in church for decades but had never had a personal encounter with someone who was homeless. Fortunately, they trusted me enough to follow through with the meal. On Sunday evening, we fed the people in the shelter, and then we sat and ate with them, listening to their stories. One woman in my group reflected on the evening, "When I looked into their faces, I saw Christ." Jesus was revealed to us in the breaking of the bread (cf Luke 24:35).

When we apply the scriptures to our own lives, when the things that matter to God matter to us, the kingdom of heaven comes to earth. Let's put away our attacks against those we don't like and embrace God and one another in Christian love. May it be in our community as it is in heaven!

#2: We Water Down the Gospel
When We Exclusively Use the Concept
Of Penal Substitution

(Penal: relating to punishment)

Hebrews 2:10-15

10 It was fitting that God, for whom and through whom all things exist, in bringing many children to glory, should make the pioneer of their salvation perfect through sufferings. 11 For the one who sanctifies and those who are sanctified all have one Father. For this reason Jesus is not ashamed to call them brothers and sisters, 12 saying,

"I will proclaim your name to my brothers and sisters, in the midst of the congregation I will praise you."

13 And again,

"I will put my trust in him."

And again,

"Here am I and the children whom God has given me."

14 Since, therefore, the children share flesh and blood, he himself likewise shared the same things, so that through death he might destroy the one who has the power of death, that is, the devil, 15 and free those who all their lives were held in slavery by the fear of death.

Prayer

Lord Jesus, thank you for becoming one of us. Thank you for fighting the fight we could never win. Thank you for conquering evil and for sharing your victory with us. Help us to celebrate our Father's love and share it freely with others. Amen.

Jesus saves us! But how? The answer matters, because it tells us something about who God is, and who God is matters. It affects our relationship with God, and it affects how we share God with others. What is it about Jesus' life, death, and resurrection that sets us free?

For the last 1000 years, the western church has gravitated toward one explanation, one theory of atonement, Anselm's Satisfaction Theory. The theologian Anselm (1033-1109) who was Archbishop of Canterbury after the Norman conquests, developed a theory of the cross rooted in the feudal system. In his world, serfs worked on the estate of an overlord, a knight. The knight protected the serfs from attack, and, in exchange, the serfs owed the knight a debt of honor. Anselm viewed God as an overlord to whom we owe a debt of honor which we have failed to sufficiently give. That failure represents sin. The only remedy for that sin is to repay the debt of honor. Since humans already owe God everything, it's impossible for us to do any more to repay the debt. Only God is capable of repaying the debt, but God didn't owe it. So, for Anselm, God became human, and through his death and resurrection paid the debt of honor owed to God. This theory can be summed up in a praise song I learned as a teenager.

> He paid the debt he did not owe.
> I owe a debt I could not pay.
> I needed someone to wash my sins away,
> And now I sing a brand-new song, Amazing Grace.
> Christ Jesus paid the debt that only He could pay.

According to Anselm, Jesus' death and resurrection earned a superabundance of merit, supererogation, and His extra merit is applied to cover the deficit of the faithful. Christ paid our debt on our behalf.

With the arrival of Protestant Reformation in 1517, Anselm's theory evolved (or maybe more accurately devolved) into the penal substitution theory, which suggests that Jesus was punished in our place, that He is our substitute. I've used this theory to explain my own faith and to try to evangelize others for years. I explained it this way. "Imagine that you're a child who's been caught doing something terrible. Your father is preparing to punish you, the old-fashioned way, with a thorough spanking. Before justice can be rendered, your older brother, who is innocent, steps in and offers to take your place, receiving the punishment for what you did." This analogy represents penal substitution and can be helpful—to a point. It is supported by scripture, "For our sake he made him to be sin who knew no sin, so that in him we might become the righteousness of God" (II Corinthians 5:21). That verse validates the idea that Jesus became our sin and that through His sacrifice our sin died. Jesus traded us His righteousness for our sin. I certainly don't want to throw away that idea entirely. It's worked for thousands of people. The church has successfully used this theory for generations to lead people to faith in Christ.

But, the theory raises some serious concerns and actually pushes some people away from God. It highlights God's wrath rather than God's grace. People have often told me that they like the idea of Jesus. He sounds really nice, but the idea of the Father scares them. The penal substitution theory does a good job of illustrating how Jesus saves us—but from whom? God? From whom are we in danger? The Father? Why would we need to be rescued from a loving God? When we consider what penal substitution says about the Father, we see an older brother taking a beating from an angry father while the younger brother runs out of the room in fear.

The penal substitution theory focuses more on a God of anger than a God of grace. In doing so, it puts God the Father and God the Son at odds with one another, the former holding us captive until the latter can rescue us. That model is particularly difficult for those who have suffered abuse. How are victims of abuse ever to relate to this God who kills His only Son, no matter how benevolent the reasons. It's been said that when you make a half-truth into a whole truth, you get an untruth. That statement is true in this case to the extent that the penal substation theory impugns the character of God. To claim that penal substitution is the whole truth about the cross is an untruth! The mean god it describes dissuades many people from believing the Gospel. After trying to believe for years, they've finally said, "No," to this bullying god.

Sadly, too many churches cling to this idea of an angry God who is constantly out to get you. Their only offer of rescue is an innocent child who got in the way of his father's anger. It's as if John 3:16 reads, "For God so hated the world that he killed his own Son to save it." But, John doesn't say that. It says, "For God so loved the world." People in those churches counter by saying that God sacrificed His Son to save us because of how much God loves us, but that idea doesn't help much. It's just the abuser justifying the abuse. Surely, we can talk about the cross in ways that don't villainize God. Surely there are ways of faithfully dealing with the crucifixion that allow us to preserve the goodness of God's nature, theories that reflect God's defining characteristic of love. Fortunately, the church has never required adherence to one specific theory of atonement. There is no orthodox view of the cross. We water down the Gospel when we exclusively use the concept of penal substitution to explain the Gospel.

There is another way of looking at the cross that dates back to the early church. Origen (c. 185 – c. 254) helped develop the ransom theory of atonement, which was widely embraced by leaders across the eastern and western church including Athanasius, Gregory of Nyssa, Gregory of Nazianzus, John Chrysostom, Ambrose, Leo the Great, Gregory the Great, and Augustine of Hippo. The *Catholic Encyclopedia* quotes Augustine on the theory.

> The Redeemer came and the deceiver was
> overcome. What did our Redeemer do to our
> Captor? In payment for us He set the trap, His
> Cross, with His blood for bait. He [Satan]
> could indeed shed that blood; but he deserved
> not to drink it. By shedding the blood of One
> who was not his debtor, he was forced to
> release his debtors.

In this theory, Father and Son work in concert to defeat the enemy. The cross is a rescue mission more than an act of judgement.

Since 1931, there has been a resurgence in the ransom theory, only slightly modified and renamed as the Christus Victor theory, (Christ the Victor). The name change is helpful. In our economic system, the word ransom has a monetary connotation. Considered this way, paying ransom too closely resembles Anselm's theory. Christus Victor more accurately represents the intentions of the Early Fathers. The cross is not a business transaction, but a rescue drama. Forgive the crude analogy, but Christus Victor reminds me a little of *Rambo*. In those movies, American soldiers are still being held captive by the enemy in Vietnam. Rambo (Sylvester Salone) goes to Vietnam, enters into their world (incarnation), suffers violence, and ultimately leads the captives to freedom from the enemy. Of course, Rambo's tactics are much more violent than those of the Prince of Peace, but the plot line is somewhat similar.

The Bible begins with a story of our first parents living in perfect peace in the Garden of Eden. All is well until they succumb to the temptations of the enemy. The crafty serpent shows up to offer them a deal. He deceives them into disobeying God, and the enemy takes humanity captive. The results of choosing evil are obvious. Thorns grow up from the ground invading the crops God provided to feed people. Work gets harder, requiring toil and sweat. Childbearing becomes painful. Evil took humanity captive. The enemy abducted God's perfect creation.

Early in the Gospels, God arrives on the planet on a rescue mission, and almost as early, evil begins to pursue God. The Incarnation is God's rescue mission to recover kidnapped family, a mission that evil intends to thwart. God puts on flesh in Bethlehem. In an effort to derail the mission, evil moves Herod to murder all the baby boys under two years old. The stage is set for an epic clash between good and evil.

Throughout Jesus's ministry, He lures evil to the cross. He intentionally breaks religious laws, healing on the Sabbath, gathering food on the Sabbath, and associating with "unclean" people. Those actions provoke the religious elite, prompting them into action to protect their power and privilege. Evil does not surrender easily. Jesus challenges civil authority claiming to be a King ushering in a new kingdom, words that would rile up the violent Roman authorities. The Trinity set a trap for the enemy. Father, Son, and Holy Spirit conspired to come on a mission to rescue those of us held captive by sin! Jesus' ministry lured evil to the cross and tempted it to claim a victory it could not hold.

By submitting to death, Jesus allowed evil to do its very worst. It wasn't the Father who put Jesus on the cross, but the enemy. The atonement is not a story of the Father punishing the Son on our behalf, but of the Trinity suffering together in an act of perfect love that would forever destroy death. Then, Jesus rose from the dead that "he might destroy the one who has the power of death, that is, the devil, and free those who all their lives were held in slavery by the fear of death" (Hebrews 2:14-15).

Jesus won the ultimate victory over evil. Because He won, we can win too. Because Christ is Victor, we too are victors, and it's evident all around us. When the church feeds hungry people, evil is defeated, and we share in Jesus' victory. When people follow Christ into our schools to offer love, support, and guidance, the enemy again suffers defeat. When God's people visit the sick and imprisoned, they claim the victory won at Calvary.

There are over 70 senior citizens in the Tuscaloosa area who are all alone. Many of them are in nursing homes. Others are waiting to be admitted. For them, days turn into weeks, and weeks into months. Birthdays come and go. No one visits. No one celebrates. That kind of loneliness is evil. Last December, I watched my church family prepare Christmas gifts for those lonely people: candy, clothes, toiletries, and other gifts and necessities. For 20 years, Forest Lake United Methodist has remembered these people who are too often forgotten. This year, we're expanding our ministry, working to provide for those people throughout the year. Evil doesn't get to win! The war was decided at Calvary, and Christ is Victor!

Christ showed us the way to defeat evil. Because He wins, we also win. His life offers the blueprint for our own. Jesus became what we are so that we can become what He is.

#1: We Water Down the Gospel
When We Invite People to Trust Jesus
For the Afterlife—But Not This Life

I John 5:11-12
11 And this is the testimony: God gave us eternal life, and this life is in his Son. 12 Whoever has the Son has life; whoever does not have the Son of God does not have life.

Prayer

Lord Jesus, too often we have chosen not to live until after we die. We've limited your most precious gift to the afterlife. Resurrect us today. Give us eternal life, now. Help us to live in your kingdom in this world so that we will be prepared for the kingdom that is still coming. Amen.

One Sunday morning during worship, a preacher, trying to gin up the excitement in the congregation, asked, "Who all here wants to go to heaven?" Everyone in the sanctuary raised their hands high in the air, except for one elderly gentleman sitting in the back pew. The preacher noticed the man's negative response. So, he asked again, even louder, "Who all here wants to go to heaven?" Again, every hand in the room went up, except for the gentleman in the back row. Thinking the man was hard of hearing, the preacher yelled, "Who all here wants to go to heaven?" Once again, every hand raised except for the one man at the back of the room. His response greatly troubled the preacher, so much so that he couldn't continue his sermon without checking on the state of the man's soul. Walking down the aisle, the preacher asked the man who wouldn't raise his hand, "Haven't you heard me ask who wants to go to heaven?"

"Yes, I have," the man answered.

"And, you haven't raised your hand once?"

"No," replied the man.

The preacher continued, "I don't understand. Don't you want to go to heaven when you die?"

The man chuckled, "Of course I want to go to heaven when I die, but I thought you were getting up a trip for right now."

That joke reminds me of the Kenney Chesney song, "Everybody Wants to Go to Heaven, But Nobody Wants to Go Now." It also reminds me of the church where the message frequently centers around what happens after you die. We've misrepresented eternal life, and we preachers carry a lot of the blame. We use the afterlife in our efforts to leverage you into a decision. We paint graphic images of the horrors of hell where sinners will roast over open fires. By contrast, for those who will respond to our message, we offer stories of a white fluffy place, a land of an unclouded day, where no storm clouds gather, and sorrow and mourning flee away. Preachers, trying to influence people to follow Jesus have inadvertently reduced His message to selling fire insurance. "Turn or burn!" When we primarily focus on the afterlife, we reduce Christianity to a transactional experience, and we reduce the church to a travel agency where people purchase their tickets for the Gospel train that will transport them to heaven's shores.

Nowhere is this approach more apparent than in many of our door to door evangelistic efforts. Strangers show up on the doorstep. People we've never met before ask us a most personal question. "If you were to die tonight, do you know where you'd go?" The last time someone asked me that question, I answered, "The funeral home." He didn't know quite how to take that response. Those interactions clearly highlight how the church has made Christianity about what happens when you die. We've postponed eternal life until a later time.

To be fair, the church's focus on the afterlife has been good for business. A few years ago, Jerry Jenkins and Tim LaHaye introduced us to the *Left Behind* series. These books tantalized us with fantastic stories about Christ's return. The faithful are mysteriously whisked away from living rooms, shopping malls, and even planes, leaving their clothes behind. The faithless were left behind where they tried to discover the reason for the disappearances. The books were wildly popular, selling millions of copies and giving rise to a matching children's series. The books were so popular, in fact, that the authors began adding fictional material to extend the series and sell more volumes. *Left Behind* became the text for Bible studies and the literature for Sunday school classes across the country. The books whetted our appetite for escaping the evils of this world to finally enjoy the goodness of heaven. We couldn't wait to get off the planet. Church became the NASA of the spiritual life.

Obsession with the afterlife is deeply rooted in the church culture. After being appointed to a new church, I picked up a copy of their hymnal to plan our first worship service. I wanted to open worship with a hymn of praise, something that would call to mind God's attributes, something like "Holy, Holy, Holy," or "Joyful, Joyful We Adore Thee." I began at the front of their hymnal, thumbing through its pages for our hymn of praise. The first 148 pages (half the hymnal) contained hymns primarily devoted to the afterlife! Hoping for heaven was more important that praising God.

It's what I've dubbed evacuation theology, an obsession with leaving this world behind in hopes of enjoying a better world in the afterlife. Evacuation theology was a foundation of my belief system in high school and college. The Revelation was my favorite book of the Bible. I dug into it to discover the mystery of how this world will end and how to guarantee my position in the afterlife. My friends and I became fascinated with the Rapture, an event in which we believed Jesus would return a call us up to heaven while we're still alive. In college, we prayed for the rapture. We dreamed about hearing the trumpet call and then bodily soaring up through the clouds on the way to glory. Secretly, we were kind of excited about seeing the looks on our enemies faces as they got left behind—final vindication for our side! Our mantra was, "Come quickly, Lord Jesus!"

I still remember the night in my dorm room when the consequences of that prayer hit home. If Jesus were to actually answer my prayer, if He hastened His return to get me out of here, there might in fact be others who would be left behind. It occurred to me that to ask Jesus to evacuate me early is to ask Him to leave others behind. Evacuation theology is a theology of exclusion. How wrong-headed of me! I was so heavenly minded that I was no earthly good.

Obsession with the afterlife can cause us to miss the message of Jesus. Over and over He preached, "Repent, for the kingdom of heaven is at hand." When He commissioned His disciples to preach, He sent them with the same message. The kingdom of heaven is not just a future promise, a reward for a good life in this work. For Jesus, the kingdom of heaven is a present reality! John tells us, "Whoever has the Son has life." present tense, not future promise. The moment we begin to follow Jesus we have eternal life. If we have the Son, we are living in eternity now. It's not just a duration of life but a quality of life. Christ followers live a different kind of life.

Of course, the Bible does teach of a heaven that comes later, a place where the streets are lined with gold and the gates made of pearl, where the saints will cast down golden crowns around a glassy sea. In that place, there'll be no sun or moon for light, for God will be the light. On the night before the crucifixion, Jesus promised that He was going to prepare a place for us. He made a promise of a heavenly home.

Jesus prefaces His promise of an eternal dwelling place with words of instruction, "Do not let your hearts be troubled" (John 14:1a). Jesus does offer is a promise of heaven but connects it to a command, "Don't worry about it." So, like the stubborn creatures we are, we've spent 2000 years worrying about it, obsessing over it, and letting it obscure the very heart of the Gospel. I'm grateful that we have a future reward, a heaven to anticipate, but why wait? Why put off eternal life when the Bible says we can have it now? We water down the Gospel when we invite people to trust Jesus for the afterlife—but not this life.

Jesus presented Christianity as a present reality more than a future hope. When the disciples asked Jesus to teach them to pray, He included in the prayer, "Thy kingdom come. Thy will be done on earth as it is in heaven." The Incarnation is an invasion of earth by heaven. The work of the kingdom is to create heaven on earth. Too much of the church has sounded retreat and is organizing for evacuation. Louis Evely makes the point beautifully in this quote from *In the Christian Spirit*.

> To believe in God is to believe in the salvation of the world. The paradox of our time is that those who believe in God do not believe in the salvation of the world, and those who believe in the future of the world do not believe in God.
>
> Christians believe in "the end of the world," they expect the final catastrophe, the punishment of others.
>
> Atheists in their turn invent doctrines of salvation, try to give meaning to life, work, the future of humankind, and refuse to believe in God because Christians believe in him and take no interest in the world.

All ignore the true God: He who has so loved the world! But which is the more culpable ignorance?

To love God is to love the world. To love God passionately is to love the world passionately. To hope in God is to hope for the salvation of the world.

I often say to myself that, in our religion, God must feel very much alone: for is there anyone besides God who believes in the salvation of the world? God seeks among us sons and daughters who resemble him enough that he could send them into the world to save it.

I believe there are those who resemble God enough for God to send them into the world to save it! We can be those Christ followers who love God enough to love the world as God loves it!

I started this chapter with a joke about a preacher. His question is valid for us. "Who all here wants to go to heaven?" In fact, Christ invites us, today to go to heaven. It's right outside our doors. Do you want to go to heaven? Get up. Go to your local food bank or soup kitchen and volunteer. You'll meet Jesus, there. You'll have the opportunity to feed Jesus a meal, maybe even eat with Him. He may not look like you'd expect. His hair might be long, stringy and oily. Her skin might be dirty and a different color than you'd imagined. He probably won't look like the painting of sexy, white Jesus hanging in your Sunday school room. But, as you hand Jesus a tray of food, you'll taste a little bit of heaven.

Do you want to go to heaven? It's as near as your local school. Churches like to complain about the absence of prayer in school. We make it the subject of our sermons. We like to blame the absence of prayer in schools for all kinds of disasters: hurricanes, forest fires, and COVID-19. I'm sick of our complaints! Rather than debate prayer in schools, Christ followers take the kingdom to campuses every day. Do you want to go to heaven? Get up. Go volunteer to help a child learn to read or do math. Take a gift to one of our hard-working, under-appreciated schoolteachers. Jesus had a special place in His heart for children. He made room for them in a culture that ignored them. When you help a child, you're helping Jesus. Take the risk of going to a place that doesn't allow prayer, and you'll discover Jesus in the eyes of a child!

Heaven is as near as the closest hospital, nursing home, or prison. You will find Christ in restaurants, stores, and even bars. Whenever we take the opportunity to love and serve other human beings, we are loving and serving Christ. "Truly I tell you, just as you did it to one of the least of these who are members of my family, you did it to me" (Matthew 25:40b).

Let's stop watering down the Gospel. Let's give up our obsession with the afterlife. I'm certain that if we're busy building the kingdom of heaven here and now, we won't have to worry about it later. Let's go to heaven, today!

Part Two:
Washed Clean

Repent

Matthew 4:12-23

12 Now when Jesus heard that John had been arrested, he withdrew to Galilee. 13 He left Nazareth and made his home in Capernaum by the sea, in the territory of Zebulun and Naphtali, 14 so that what had been spoken through the prophet Isaiah might be fulfilled:

15 "Land of Zebulun, land of Naphtali,
    on the road by the sea, across the Jordan, Galilee of the Gentiles—

16 the people who sat in darkness
    have seen a great light,
and for those who sat in the region and shadow of death
    light has dawned."

17 From that time Jesus began to proclaim, "Repent, for the kingdom of heaven has come near."

18 As he walked by the Sea of Galilee, he saw two brothers, Simon, who is called Peter, and Andrew his brother, casting a net into the sea—for they were fishermen. 19 And he said to them, "Follow me, and I will make you fish for people." 20 Immediately they left their nets and followed him. 21 As he went from there, he saw two other brothers, James son of Zebedee and his brother John, in the boat with their father Zebedee, mending their nets, and he called

them. 22 Immediately they left the boat and their father, and followed him.

23 Jesus went throughout Galilee, teaching in their synagogues and proclaiming the good news of the kingdom and curing every disease and every sickness among the people.

Prayer

Lord Jesus, forgive us for shouting, "Repent!" at the world without practicing repentance ourselves. Give us grace to turn away from loveless ways and to turn toward loving ways. Today, may we drop our own agendas and follow you. Amen.

REPENT! Too often, we've used the word as a weapon to attack those with whom we disagree. We point our fingers at an unbelieving generation and yell, "Repent, you evil doers. Be like us." We follow the attack with a threat of eternal torment if they fail to comply. (And, we're surprised that this method no longer works.)

The word "repent" reminds me of an encounter from my sophomore year in college. In the 80s, there was a lectern in front of the Ferguson Center, our student union building, that was available for anyone to share whatever message might be on her or his heart. On this particular afternoon, as I was walking to my dorm, there was an aggressive young preacher desperately trying to save all of us from our sins. I admired his courage, but was put off by his tone. He sounded so angry. He yelled at us students as we passed by. He called us out on our sins, naming the things he assumed we had done. To be fair, we were undergraduate students at the University of Alabama. Certainly, there were some sins in the crowd to be attacked. After accusing us of drunkenness, fornication, and a host of other sins, he yelled at us to repent or burn. By the way he was preaching his message, I was convinced he was hoping that we would burn, kind of like when Jonah fantasized about the destruction of Nineveh. I hope his message was helpful for some. Personally, I felt more abused than loved, more attacked than welcomed. As I walked on to my dorm, I wondered if that's the way we Christians sound to the world around us.

I didn't like my answer. It's not just the street preacher. I'm afraid that we're all tempted to use repentance as a weapon against people we don't like. We may not be so bold and aggressive as the young preacher from the Ferguson Center, but we easily fall into the trap of publicly pointing out others' sins while quietly ignoring our own. Perhaps it's the reason why so many accuse us of being judgmental. The temptation to judge is real for me!

When I was in high school, I disliked the party crowd. I was known as the "church kid" (among other names), a reputation I embraced and celebrated. It made me feel better than them. I disapproved of all the wild partiers, at least partly because I didn't fit in with them. I was convinced that *they* needed to change. *They* needed to get right. *They* needed to repent—and be more like me. *They* were the ones with the problem. I was just fine. The delusion is attractive to us church folks. Being convinced that everyone else is wrong gives us a comfortable feeling of superiority.

While claiming to live a more Biblical life, I completely missed the parts of the New Testament where Jesus was at the parties. He hung out at the homes of known sinners like Zacchaeus and Matthew. The religious officials rightly accused Jesus of being the friend of sinners. Based on my behavior in high school, I would have been complaining about Jesus, too. I would have been pointing my finger at Jesus for not being holy enough, for not being like me. I wish I could say that I outgrew my judgmentalism by high school graduation, but it doesn't die that easily. The temptation to make repentance other people's business is ever-present. I hope I'm at least better able to recognize it, now.

The temptation is never far from us because it works for us. It gives us an excuse to exclude the people we don't like. Say, for instance, we don't like people with tattoos or piercings or wild hair styles. To justify our dislike, we dig through the scriptures to find verses that, taken out of context, seem to support our biases. Suddenly, God is on our side. Convinced that God dislikes those people, we feel no obligation to include them. *They* need to change.

My argument is not hypothetical. My friends with tattoos and piercings experience the judgement from church folks all the time. One friend, who is definitely a follower of Christ, has been confronted numerous times about her tattoos. "Don't you know your body is the temple of the Holy Spirit?" chide her accusers. "Yes," she says, "and my temple has stained glass windows." I'm not telling you that you have to like tattoos. I'm not telling you to get a tattoo. I'm also not telling you not to get one. We do have to stop blaming God for our hatred of people that do things we don't like. When we decide who we don't like and twist the Bible to prove God agrees with us, we'll use repentance to prove people are wrong and fail to change what we need to change in ourselves. As long as we believe that it's other people who need to repent, we insulate ourselves from experiencing the transformation we need. If the other person is the problem, why should I change?

Since the time of Christ, the church has preached a message of repentance. It's a message we received from Jesus, Himself! It's a cornerstone of the Christian message and one of our baptismal vows. If repentance is such a good thing, why don't we Christians do more of it?

Maybe we resist repentance because we don't understand it. Biblical repentance is not an attack against perceived bad behaviors or the people who do them. It's not a threat of eternal damnation! Repentance is an invitation to kingdom living. In Greek, the original language of the New Testament, the word for repentance is *metanoia*. It's a compound word that literally means change of mind. More than just a conversion of opinion, it implies a change of behavior that coincides with the change of thinking. We might call repentance a change of heart. Encouraging someone to repent is not an attack on their current behavior but an invitation to something new.

It's not mere coincidence that the stories in this chapter's text are placed side by side. Matthew tells us that Jesus began preaching, "Repent, for the kingdom of heaven has come near." In the very next verse, He sees Peter and Andrew. The author put these two verses next to each other for a reason. Jesus' encounter with the brothers was not just the next thing to happen on a Thursday afternoon. The Gospel writers didn't tell their stories that way. Instead, they used the narrative to convey their intended message. Matthew tells us that Jesus began preaching a message of repentance. Then he immediately follows that message with two stories of what repentance in the Jesus movement looks like. Since repentance is of central importance to the Christian movement, let's see what it looked like with the first disciples.

Simon and Andrew were teenage boys following in their father's footsteps. They chose the family profession of fishing on the Sea of Galilee. They had chosen the direction for their lives. Jesus approaches them while they are casting their nets into the lake with His message of repentance. Notice, Peter and Andrew are not doing anything wrong. Fishing is an honorable profession. They're supporting their dad's business and helping to provide for the family. Jesus doesn't accuse them of bad behavior or threaten them with punishment. Instead, Jesus invites them to something new, to reorient their lives from fishing for fish to fishing for people. Upon hearing Jesus' invitation, the brothers immediately repent. They change their mind about their life's vocation, and they change their behavior. They drop their nets and follow Jesus. To make sure we get the point, Matthew immediately tells an almost identical story about James and John. Matthew wants us to see repentance in action. Repentance occurs when we encounter Jesus, we hear His call, we change our thinking, and we follow Him into His way of living.

The invitation of repentance is to turn toward Christ, but it implies a turning away from something as well. So, from what does God call us to turn? The first United Methodist baptismal vow asks us, "Do you renounce the spiritual forces of wickedness, reject the evil powers of this world, and repent of your sin?" (*United Methodist Hymnal*) At first glance, that's a no-brainer! I've never met anyone who brazenly says, "I'm choosing to align with wickedness and evil." Even the most evil characters from history generally claim noble reasons for their behaviors. Our sin is usually more subtle and much more easily disguised, sometimes to look like righteousness. At its most basic level sin (or evil) is breaking the Great Commandment which is Jesus' command to love God with our whole lives and to love our neighbors as ourselves. Sin is a failure to love. The Greek word used for love in the Great Commandment is *agape*, which is an unconditional love that can't be earned or lost. It's God's love for us when we are at our very best and our very worst. It includes both love for friends and love for enemies. This love is what Jesus commands us to have for one another.

Ironically, I've often clung to my sense of self-righteousness while hating other people. Because I considered myself the good Christian church kid, I felt justified in hating the party crowd. For too many years, my heterosexuality was an excuse to hate the LGBTQIA+ community. Claiming to be righteous, I embraced evil (failure to love) and betrayed my own calling. That kind of righteousness is Pharisaical and the Apostle Paul equates it with filthy rags.

Pharisaical righteousness sees enemies and outsiders as despicable sinners. *Agape* sees them the way God sees them, as beloved children. Being a father of three children has given me fresh insight into what a*gape* love looks like. Like most kids, mine will fight from time to time. I've even had to pull one off of the other more than once. Almost always, my children feel justified in the anger against their siblings. Each child feels he or she was right while the brother or sister was obviously in the wrong. As their father, I want peace. I wanted my kids to live in love with each other. I wanted them to repent of their evil, of their failure to love, and to choose a new path. I'm convinced that no one will be accused in the judgment of loving too much or of loving too many.

Through the message of repentance, Jesus invites us to turn from our loveless ways and to turn toward God. For years, I defined turning toward God as believing correct doctrine. I studied hard to make sure that I believed the "right" thing about the Virgin Birth, the Incarnation, the Resurrection, assurance of salvation, falling from grace, the Rapture, and many other theological topics. I'm a nerd by nature, so I treated Christianity like a test that I intended to pass with an A+. The problem with my approach is that it left a lot of room to criticize those people who had the "wrong" answers. Once I identified those with wrong beliefs, it was a short journey to disliking them, attacking them, and even hating them. Knowing the truth about God doesn't guarantee that we are following God.

Jesus doesn't invite us to a belief system. He doesn't ask us to pass a theology test. He invites us to trust Him. Almost universally, the word believe or belief in the Bible can be better translated as trust. Christ asks us to trust Him enough to follow Him, to do things His way. That's good news, because even a child can understand. A few years ago, I received a phone call from a woman in a church that I had recently served. She told me that her five-year-old son was asking questions about God and said he wanted to be a Christian. She asked if I would talk with him. I prayed a quick prayer asking for wisdom for a way to share our story with a child so young.

Then, driving down the road, on the way to make a hospital visit, I had a faith conversation with a kindergartener. He told me he believed in Jesus, and we talked about what that means. Then I ask him two questions. "Are you willing to live like Christ?" He said, "Yes!" Then I asked, "Are you willing to love like Christ?" Again, he said, "Yes!" Soon afterward, I baptized him.

Repentance is God's gift to us to turn us toward God. May we treasure the invitation and never again use it to attack another person! May we remember our baptism. Let us renew our promise to repent, to turn from loveless ways and toward loving ways. Today, we decide, with God's help, to live like Christ and love like Christ.

Resist

Romans 12:9-21

9 Let love be genuine; hate what is evil, hold fast to what is good; 10 love one another with mutual affection; outdo one another in showing honor. 11 Do not lag in zeal, be ardent in spirit, serve the Lord. 12 Rejoice in hope, be patient in suffering, persevere in prayer. 13 Contribute to the needs of the saints; extend hospitality to strangers. 14 Bless those who persecute you; bless and do not curse them. 15 Rejoice with those who rejoice, weep with those who weep. 16 Live in harmony with one another; do not be haughty, but associate with the lowly; do not claim to be wiser than you are. 17 Do not repay anyone evil for evil, but take thought for what is noble in the sight of all. 18 If it is possible, so far as it depends on you, live peaceably with all. 19 Beloved, never avenge yourselves, but leave room for the wrath of God; for it is written, "Vengeance is mine, I will repay, says the Lord." 20 No, "if your enemies are hungry, feed them; if they are thirsty, give them something to drink; for by doing this you will heap burning coals on their heads." 21 Do not be overcome by evil, but overcome evil with good.

Prayer

Lord Jesus, open our eyes that we might see the hurting people in our world. Fill our hearts with compassion that we might see them the way you see them. Fill us with the Spirit that we might have the courage to resist evil and liberate those who are oppressed. Amen

Our second United Methodist baptismal vow asks, "Do you resist evil, injustice, and oppression in whatever forms they present themselves?" That's a silly question. Who doesn't want to resist evil, injustice, and oppression? No one volunteers to promote evil! We never host volunteer recruitment days for injustice and oppression. On the surface, almost everyone would claim to oppose such negative things. So, why do we ask?

Generally, people believe they have good reasons for their actions. They claim noble causes for their ignoble behaviors. Some of the greatest evil in human history was perpetrated by Adolf Hitler. He engineered the murder of 6 million Jews and 5 million other human beings who didn't fit his ideal Arian standard. The Third Reich was a tragedy that continues to affect us decades later. From our vantage point, it's hard to see anything but the evil of the Holocaust. Yet, Hitler, deceived as he was, believed he was doing something good for his country. He considered himself to be acting as a patriot. Following World War I, the Allied Powers punished Germany severely for its role in the war. Those punitive measures led to a horrible depression in Germany. The country was in ruins without much hope for a better future. Desperation set the scene for Hitler's rise. He encouraged national pride and gave the citizens a common enemy. Under his rule, Germany did return to power on the world stage. To be sure, Adolf Hitler launched one of the most evil empires in the modern world, but he did it to save his country. He was committed to making Germany great again! Hitler demonstrates evil disguised as nationalism. Other countries knew what he was doing. Most failed to act.

We see evil all around us, too. Often, we lack the power to resist. Too often, it's too hard to stand against evil. So the church must ask, "Do you resist evil, injustice, and oppression in whatever forms they present themselves?"

Considering some examples of current injustice and oppression that might help us better understand our reluctance to resist.

Around the world, 168 million children, ages 5-14, work in sweatshops for pennies a day (www.dosomething.org). Women and girls are forced to take birth control to guarantee that they won't miss days of work due to pregnancy or childcare. Children work 12 hour shifts without the possibility of education. It's a system that guarantees the perpetuation of poverty, hunger, and homelessness. The practice is evil. I don't know one person who would encourage her or his child to work in a sweatshop. Yet, the practice continues. We live in the most powerful nation in the history of the world, but we're somehow powerless to stop it. Why? Why is such evil allowed to continue? How do we turn our heads when millions of children are treated as disposable? The answer, at least in part, is that we like cheap merchandise. There is a financial cost to ending sweatshop labor. Pay workers a living wage, and our clothes will cost more. So, sweatshops continue. And the church must ask, "Do you resist evil, injustice, and oppression in whatever forms they present themselves?" Perhaps, faithfulness to our baptismal vows will require that we by ethical and sustainable clothing. It is available, if we're willing to pay the cost.

The cocoa fields on the Ivory Coast in Africa are populated with hundreds of small cocoa farms. Most of the workers are children ages 12-18. These kids should be in school, playing sports, dating, falling in love, and dreaming about their futures. Instead, they swing machetes all day long. They're forced to spray dangerous pesticides that threaten their health and their future. They have no opportunity for education, and making only pennies per week, no hope of ever breaking free from this form of modern-day slavery. Many of these children work on their parent's farms, but at least 16,000 are working on non-family farms where they were sold into labor. For 20 years, candy companies like Hershey and Mars have promised to improve conditions, but the promises have largely been empty. In a recent interview, one executive admitted that they don't even know where half of the farms are that produce their cocoa. No one supports that kind of child labor. No one advocates for slavery. These examples represent pure evil. Yet, it continues unchecked. Why are such obvious abuses of humanity ignored? Why don't we resist? We like cheap Milky Ways! Paying a decent wage would increase our candy cost at Halloween! So, the church must ask, "Do you resist evil, injustice, and oppression in whatever forms they present themselves?" Even if it means paying higher prices for chocolate?

Of course, oppression is not just a foreign problem. We struggle with it in the "land of the free and home of the brave." Currently, our country imprisons children in cages because they were born on the wrong side of an invisible line. Their parents brought them here illegally. It wasn't the children's choice. By law, we separate children from parents and lock them up. In too many cases, we've been unable to reunite children with their parents even in their home country. Perpetrators argue that they're just following the law, a common defense offered by SS Guards at Nuremburg. Stripping children from their parents and caging them is evil! Why do we tolerate it in a country that prides itself on freedom? We allow it because we're afraid. We fear that immigrants might take our jobs. We're afraid that immigrants are dangerous, even though they commit fewer violent crimes than Americans. We allow evil to protect our way of life. So, the church must ask, "Do you resist evil, injustice, and oppression in whatever forms they present themselves?"

These problems are complicated, and their solutions will be equally complicated! To even talk about them makes us uncomfortable. We'd rather not know that such evil exists. But, to ignore it is to participate in it, for these and other evils thrive on our ignorance. Our baptismal vows call us to make a difference. But, resistance will come at a cost. A just world will possibly cost me some of my privilege. Is my baptism worth it?

"Do you resist evil, injustice, and oppression in whatever forms they present themselves?" It's a tough question because it requires a tough answer. Do we hate evil enough to sacrifice to resist it? None of us will fix these problems on our own, but are we willing to resist?

Let's start today. Read the passage from Romans 12, again. Pray for God to open your eyes to ways that we fail to live up to that Christian standard. Ask yourself these questions. "What breaks my heart? What causes my fists to clinch?" When you identify what makes you sad and mad, you might have identified where Christ calls you to work. Maybe your calling will be poverty or hunger, maybe homelessness or civil rights for marginalized people. It's probably not possible to work faithfully in every area, but we can, we must take a stand somewhere. Start today by discovering your calling and taking your stand—no matter the cost!

Confess

John 6:36-40

²⁶ Jesus answered them, "Very truly, I tell you, you are looking for me, not because you saw signs, but because you ate your fill of the loaves. ²⁷ Do not work for the food that perishes, but for the food that endures for eternal life, which the Son of Man will give you. For it is on him that God the Father has set his seal." ²⁸ Then they said to him, "What must we do to perform the works of God?" ²⁹ Jesus answered them, **"This is the work of God, that you believe in <u>him</u> whom he has sent."** ³⁰ So they said to him, "What sign are you going to give us then, so that we may see it and believe you? What work are you performing? ³¹ Our ancestors ate the manna in the wilderness; as it is written, 'He gave them bread from heaven to eat.'" ³² Then Jesus said to them, "Very truly, I tell you, it was not Moses who gave you the bread from heaven, but it is my Father who gives you the true bread from heaven. ³³ For the bread of God is that which comes down from heaven and gives life to the world." ³⁴ They said to him, "Sir, give us this bread always." ³⁵ Jesus said to them, "I am the bread of life. Whoever comes to me will never be hungry, and whoever believes in me will never be thirsty. ³⁶ But I said to you that you have seen me and yet do not believe. ³⁷ Everything that the Father gives me will come to me, and anyone who comes to me I will never drive away; ³⁸ for I have come down from

heaven, not to do my own will, but the will of him who sent me. [39] And this is the will of him who sent me, that I should lose nothing of all that he has given me, but raise it up on the last day. [40] This is indeed the will of my Father, that all who see the Son and believe in him may have eternal life; and I will raise them up on the last day." (emphasis added)

Prayer

Lord Jesus, give us, by the power of your Holy Spirit, the ability to believe where we have not seen. Help us to trust in you that we might receive eternal life both now and in the life to come. Amen.

"Believe and be saved!" Don't believe and…well, lack of belief is frequently accompanied by threats of fire and brimstone with weeping and gnashing of teeth. To avoid that horrible punishment and gain the promise of heaven, preachers have encouraged and even threatened us to believe—but believe what? From our early years, many of us were taught to believe the Bible. The written word of God has become the foundation for belief. Many of us were taught that it is inerrant and taught to stake our eternities on the validity of the words written in its pages. "Just believe the Bible" sounds great until you actually read it. Then, the problems begin.

For me, it was in elementary school. Sunday school classes, sermons, and Vacation Bible School programs worked hard to indoctrinate me in scriptural truth. I learned how God created the earth and all that is in it in six days, a miracle which occurred about 6000 years ago. Church taught me that the stories of Genesis chapters one and two, which I mysteriously wove into a single narrative, were God's infallible word that I must accept by faith if I really believed in God. To reject the creation story was to reject the faith. To challenge it was to question God's word and seen as a weakness of faith. I was fine with my Biblical "science" lessons until third grade, when I fell in love with dinosaurs. Like many children, I was amazed by the stories of brontosauruses, pterodactyls, and of course the mighty tyrannosaurus rex. Fossils intrigued me. When my class went to the library, I made a beeline for the science section. My fascination with science led to my very first crisis of faith. Genesis failed to mention dinosaurs, and their historical timeline didn't fit my church training. According to scientists, those massive lizards lived millions of years before the Genesis creation. I remember lying in my bed at night trying to reconcile the two, convinced that, somehow, both must be right. My faith crisis hit a pinnacle one afternoon on the school bus. We were talking about what we wanted to be when we grew up. I said, "I want to be a scientist." The boy sitting next to me responded with a look of shock, "I thought you were a Christian." Apparently, I would have to choose one or the other. My confusion only deepened in the summer after my third-grade year when my family went to Washington D.C. I was thrilled to visit the Smithsonian Institution, amazed by the wonders lined up one after another. I walked around the massive brontosaurus skeleton, awe-struck, but I was convinced that the scientists had somehow completely messed up the timeline (by a few million years.)

The challenge of "just believing the Bible" extends beyond the creation stories. Read just a few pages further to discover the oldest man in the scriptures, Methuselah, who lived to be 969 years old.

That story certainly strains belief, so much so that many have offered the idea that years might have been shorter way back then. Read further in the Old Testament to discover the story of Jonah, a man who was swallowed by a fish, lived three days in its belly, and was vomited up near Nineveh where he proceeded to preach a sermon that saved the city. Science, of course, argues that no fish exists which could swallow a person whole. But, if you want to be saved, you have to believe the Bible. Science must be wrong.

All of these challenges to believing the Bible are posed by *elementary school science*! The church's fixation on Biblical inerrancy requires 9-year-old children to make a choice between science and faith. Faith is losing at an increasing rate! The church is failing to reach new generations in part because it treats the Bible as God. It has become the object of our faith. To it, we swear allegiance. We even have a pledge for it! I worked in a Christian school where every chapel service began with a "Pledge of Allegiance to the Bible." The requirement to believe the whole Bible is so central to much of American Christianity, that one of my members told me, "I believe the whole Bible, preacher, every word of it. I may not have read it, but I believe it!" Treating the Bible as though it were God is a form of idolatry. I fear that we are worshipping the book rather than it's Author!

So, what are we supposed to believe? As my journey continued, I ignored the problems posed by science, assuming that God would somehow make sense out of those Bible passages in the next life. I turned my attention toward theological concerns. During my junior high and high school years, I worked to develop my understanding of salvation. I learned what verses would help to explain new life and help me lead others to it. I embraced the idea of penal substitution that we discussed earlier in the book. During that same time, I developed a deep appreciation for the sacraments: baptism and holy communion. As a lifelong Methodist, I rooted my beliefs in free will, and I trained myself for debates with my Baptists friends over "once saved, always saved." By my college years, I fancied myself an apologist, ready to defend the faith against all those with "wrong" beliefs. As a 20-year-old, I had buried my concerns about Biblical inerrancy under a host of theological debates. If I couldn't be sure about certain Bible stories, I could at least be solid on doctrine.

Developing sound doctrine is a good thing. I encourage it. As a pastor, I try to offer opportunities for people to further develop their doctrine. But, just like the Bible shouldn't be our object of belief, neither should "correct" doctrine. In fact, obsession with doctrinal purity carries some inherent dangers. We'll consider two.

First, convinced of the certainty of our doctrine, we have too easy an excuse to point fingers at those who believe the "wrong" things. We may think that we have theological grounds for attacking others that are heretics. Unfortunately, the church has a long history of such attacks. We have arrested, imprisoned, exiled, and executed those we deemed to be heretics. These kinds of attacks expose our arrogance. We believe in a God who created this massive, beautiful, intricate universe. How can we claim to have figured out such a God? How can we claim expertise over a God so beyond our wildest imaginations? The church already has too much blood on its hands. It's time we learn the way of love and quit brutalizing people (physically, emotionally, and spiritually) for disagreeing with us!

Second, obsession with doctrinal purity trust in the Bible will ultimately fail us in a crisis. Easy answers won't work in tough times. Maybe the crisis is caused by scripture, itself, like discovering that our God of love ordered the genocide of entire nations. According to Deuteronomy 7, God demands the annihilation of seven nations.

> 1 When the Lord your God brings you into the land that you are about to enter and occupy, and he clears away many nations before you—the Hittites, the Girgashites, the Amorites, the Canaanites, the Perizzites, the Hivites, and the Jebusites, seven nations mightier and more numerous than you— 2 and when the Lord your God gives them over to you and you defeat them, then *you must utterly destroy them.* Make no covenant with them and *show them no mercy.* (NRSV emphasis added)

My previous struggles with creation and Jonah taught me not to ask critical questions of passages like this one. For many others, though, examples like this are enough reason to reject Christianity because they refuse to stake their belief on a story like this one. When the Bible is the foundation of belief, these stories are a threat to faith. Doctrinal purity doesn't account for this violent depiction of God.

Maybe the crisis is intellectual, like discovering that creation took much longer than six days. The crisis might be historical, like discovering that the church murdered people for believing the "wrong" thing. Very often, our crises are personal.

When I was four years old, my uncle was diagnosed with lung cancer. I have shadowy memories of him taking my brothers and me to the beach, of him playing with us in his backyard, and of him taking us to church. While I don't remember the details of his illness, my family tells me how godly a man my uncle was and of the hundreds of people who prayed for his healing. The Bible says that God will heal. "Are any among you sick? They should call for the elders of the church and have them pray over them, anointing them with oil in the name of the Lord. The prayer of faith will save the sick, and the Lord will raise them up; and anyone who has committed sins will be forgiven" (James 5:14-15). They believed the Bible, the Apostle's Creed, and the teaching of the church. My uncle died anyway.

For many who trust their belief in the Bible and doctrine, these kinds of crises cause them to walk away from the faith. I was afraid that accepting scientific reality would cause my faith to collapse like a house of cards. Even questioning my uncle's death might lead to questioning the foundations of Christianity. Trusting an inerrant Bible and doctrinal purity leads to a debilitating fear. If some of what I believed wasn't true, maybe none of it was true. If I'm wrong about one thing, maybe I'm wrong about everything. If I'm wrong about creation, maybe I'm wrong about the resurrection. Trusting doctrine encourages the slippery slope theory that suggests challenging one thing causes a person to slide all the way to the bottom where there will be utter destruction. The slippery slope is only a danger when we put our trust in the wrong place.

What if my approach to belief was wrong? What if the foundation of Christianity is not a book or a belief system? Jesus didn't ask us to believe *things*. He didn't offer us a creed, a vision statement, or a list of core values. He never asked the disciples to submit a theological thesis nor did He require a litmus test on key issues. Jesus asked us to believe in Him. "This is the work of God, that you believe in him whom he has sent." The foundation of our belief is not a what, but a who! Faith that is built on things and ideas will ultimately fail us. Our strength is not in our knowledge of the Bible, our knowledge of church history, or our correct belief system. While all these are important, our trust must be in Christ alone!

The Greek work used in our text for "believe" is *pisteuo*. It expresses reliance more than mere credence. It is better translated as trust. In fact, throughout the New Testament, we would be better served if we translated the word belief as trust. What Jesus asked of us is an all-in, comprehensive trust in who He is. When my son Michael was just two or three years old, a friend and I used to toss him back and forth through the air. I held Michael, facing away from me, and threw him across the room to my friend who turned him around and threw him back. Michael giggled and laughed. He couldn't get enough of it. We'd throw him until we were exhausted. Still, he would hold his hands up to me and ask, "Again?" (Fortunately, I never dropped him, as evidenced by the fact that I'm here to write these words.) Michael gives us a beautiful picture of faith. He flew through the air without a care in the world, because he knew daddy would catch him. He trusted! Jesus invites us to that kind of faith, to launch ourselves through this world into the arms of Someone we know will catch us.

That kind of belief, that kind of trust makes all the difference in our faith! Trusting Christ gives us strength in the face of crisis. Sometimes the Bible doesn't make sense. It doesn't behave the way that I think it ought to behave. When the Bible troubles me, and it does, I can still trust Jesus. Even if the Bible fails me, like in third grade, Christ will catch me.

Sometimes, I pray for someone's healing, and he or she dies. I don't know why some recover while I'm left to do funerals for others. Nothing in my training offers a satisfactory answer. Still, I trust Jesus. Trusting God for what I can't understand works for me!

Sometimes, I come across belief systems that are troubling to me. I'm tempted to point out where they're wrong, because, of course, I must be right! I'm learning to just love people and trust Jesus who's reconciling *all* things to Himself. I don't have to make the "wrong" people right, and I'm learning to admit that I might be the one in the wrong, and that's okay.

Trusting Jesus frees us to love people deeply and unconditionally! I don't have to "fix" anybody. I trust God to fix whatever might be wrong in the other person's life or in mine. My job is to love, and I hope that in my love others might see Christ.

"Do you confess Jesus Christ as your Savior, put your *whole trust* in His grace, and promise to serve Him as your Lord, in union with the church which Christ has opened to people of all ages, nations, and races?" (*The United Methodist Hymnal*, emphasis added).

www.ingramcontent.com/pod-product-compliance
Lightning Source LLC
Chambersburg PA
CBHW072016040426
42447CB00009B/1647